PRAISE FOR T...... ...

"While retelling the atrocities he witnessed, Lee is still able to retell the moments that highlight the humanity that the Khmer Rouge were unable to strip the Cambodian people of. Throughout his time living under the Khmer Rouge regime, Lee witnessed senseless beatings, killings, sexual violence, and exploitation of people yet he finds a way to see the humanity of everyone involved. Reading about the Khmer Rouge's brutality toward the people of Cambodia is gut wrenching, but Lee does a great job of sharing an inspiring story of how he and his family were able to stick together even if it meant risking their own lives. Through the misery and grief, Lee explains how he doesn't keep hate in his heart and instead chooses to come through this experience for a greater appreciation of life. Lee's perspective and outlook on life makes him a gifted and brilliant storyteller who inspires hope into those who read or listen to his story."

—**Ronak Patel** former Editor-In-Chief of the *UCA Echo*

"The powerful scenes documented in this book will stagger readers, inviting us to reckon with the unfathomable cruelty and terror of which bent, deranged humans are capable. At once, it bears testimony to the rawest brand of suffering and the triumph of resilience, and serves as a reminder that to make the highest use of dark histories, invaluable narratives, and our very humanity, perhaps our most essential duties are to read and listen."

—**Erin Wood** author of *Women Make Arkansas: Conversations with 50 Creatives*, editor of *Scars: An Anthology*, and owner of Et Alia Press

"What Kenny Duran has done here, as a writer, a listener, and a student, is not only admirable, but simultaneously humbling and inspiring. *Thank the Evil* captures trauma, dislocation, and resiliency. It captures human interactions at their best and worst. In short: it's an extraordinary, humanizing story that will stay with you long after you finish the last page."

—**Jennifer Case**, Ph.D., Assistant Professor of Creative Writing, University of Central Arkansas; author of *Sawbill: A Search for Place*

THANK THE EVIL

A SURVIVOR'S STORY
OF THE CAMBODIAN GENOCIDE

KENNY DURAN

Printed in the United States of America.

Contact the Author: kennymdauthor@gmail.com
Website: https://thanktheevil.wixsite.com/kennyduran

ISBN: 978-1-7363348-0-5 (paperback)
ISBN: 978-1-7363348-1-2 (e-book)

Library of Congress Control Number (LCCN): 2020924892

Created with the help of young Arkansas creatives:

Cover Design by Caitlyn Phan
Instagram: @creatorcaitlyn

Copy Editor: Louisa Utley
louisa.utley123@gmail.com

CONTENTS

PART 1: EVIL'S PREQUEL

Introduction 9
Meeting Mr. Lee 15
Childhood In Phnom Penh 29
Evacuation 45

PART 2: EVIL'S WORLD

Vampire Mosquitos 59
Brave Village 76
School 93
Palm Trees 116
Finding A Home 134
Chllop Team 150
The Vietnamese Invasion. 162

PART 3: EVIL'S EXODUS

Leaving Phnom Penh 185
Philippines 225

Epilogue 241
Photos 247
Bibliography 253
About The Author 257
Acknowledgements 259

PART 1
EVIL'S PREQUEL

INTRODUCTION

SALOTH SAR

IT WAS MAY 19, 1925 in the village of Prek Sbauv, Cambodia, when Saloth Sar was born. During his academic career, he studied in Cambodia's capital Phnom Penh before moving in 1948 to Paris to continue his higher education. While there, Sar was exposed to communist ideology, and in 1951, became involved with the Marxist Circle of Khmer Students in Paris. This student-led group would meet to discuss Marxist texts and the liberation of Cambodia from foreign influences. Saloth Sar remained in Paris where he joined the French Communist Party and indulged himself in communist literature until he returned to Cambodia in 1953 with the intent of sparking a revolution.

In the early 1960s, Saloth Sar and other French-educated Cambodians formed the Communist Party of Kampuchea

(CPK), also known as the Khmer Rouge. The Khmer Rouge lived in the Cambodian jungle as they observed tensions build within their country. In 1969, the United States began dropping bombs on the eastern border of Cambodia along the Ho Chi Minh trail to destroy North Vietnamese and Vietcong bases. This bombing campaign was known as Project Menu because each major bombing site was code worded with mealtimes: breakfast, lunch, snack, dinner, supper, and dessert. The Cambodian economy was already stagnating, and the constant military danger further destabilized the country. Meanwhile, Saloth Sar was hiding in the jungle enjoying the simplicity and autonomy of rural village life which furthered his dream of an idyllic communist agrarian utopia. The Khmer Rouge saw it as the true Cambodia, void of foreign influences that had subjugated the nation through imperialism and colonialism. Slowly, they began gaining influence in small village communities, but their breakthrough would not come until the start of the new decade.

On March 18, 1970, Cambodia's leader Prince Sihanouk was ousted by his political rival, Prime Minister Lon Nol and his cousin Prince Sisowith Sirik Matak, in a U.S. supported military coup. Prince Sihanouk had remained neutral amid the ongoing war in Vietnam. He permitted Vietnamese communists to set up bases in Cambodia, which ultimately led to the U.S. bombing campaigns that he did not adamantly oppose. Most rural Cambodians were outraged because they viewed Sihanouk as a god-king. Additionally, as a result of Project Menu, the Vietcong and North Vietnamese retreated further into Cambodia, thus forcing the United States to bomb more of the country. Between 1965-1973, the United States dropped more bombs on Cambodia than Allied forces dropped in all of World War II.

Saloth Sar and the Khmer Rouge used the bombings to strengthen their influence in rural villages by blaming the destruction of their communities on Americans. Their tactics, however, did not stop there. After Prince Sihanouk was ousted by Lon Nol, he fled to China and voiced his support for the Khmer Rouge. He urged the Cambodian people to revolt against Lon Nol. As a result, Sihanouk formed the National United Front of Kampuchea (FUNK), an umbrella organization for people who opposed Lon Nol. One of the key players was the Khmer Rouge, although FUNK consisted of the North Vietnamese, Viet Cong, and the Pathet Lao as well. Since the peasantry in the villages mainly supported Sihanouk, recruitment for the Khmer Rouge and FUNK became easier.

Lon Nol's coup also intensified the already ongoing Cambodian Civil War, which now pitted Lon Nol's soldiers of the Khmer Republic against the communist groups under FUNK. Lon Nol framed Vietnamese communists as the enemy and allowed the United States to fully invade Cambodia. The American bombings on the eastern border pushed the North Vietnamese and Vietcong further into the country.

The Cambodian Civil War concluded on April 17, 1975 with the Khmer Rouge victorious when they seized the capital of Phnom Penh. Saloth Sar gave himself a new name, Pol Pot, and his revolution for a communist agrarian utopia would soon become realized. Between 1975-1979, Pol Pot and his Khmer Rouge would go on to create the most infamous genocide in modern Cambodian history—with estimates of over a million people dead.

This book is a work of literary journalism about one of the survivors, Mr. Lee. I met him through his daughter, and my high school friend, Amanda Lee. It is also a Capstone project completed for the Norbert O. Schedler Honors College at the University of Central Arkansas. While interviewing Mr. Lee for this book, he and his wife owned and operated Oriental Kitchen, a small family-owned Chinese takeout restaurant. Currently, Mr. Lee and his wife are retired and reside in Conway, Arkansas.

Thank the Evil is a blend of past and present. There are scenes of my interactions with the Lee family and my travels in

Siem Reap intertwined with memories of Mr. Lee's childhood in Cambodia. Readers, I ask you all to follow my character. Together we can experience the tragic, yet resilient story of Mr. Lee during the Khmer Rouge's reign in Cambodia. His story is not just a Cambodian story, but also an American story, an Arkansan story. It is a tale told by millions of immigrants in our nation's history fleeing their perilous homelands in search of a second chance.

MEETING MR. LEE

WHY DO WE have to get boba? It's so overpriced here."
Amanda Lee turns around to face me. "This is
AMERICA… not ASIA. Boba can't be $2 here," she says. In
high school, the two of us were a bit more than acquaintances,
although we never considered each other as close friends. We
have been out of touch for a while even though we both live
in Conway and attend colleges ten minutes apart; in fact, it's
probably been a couple of years since we've last seen each other.
With the start of the first semester of my junior year rapidly
approaching, we figured it was a perfect time to reconnect
before continuing our busy lives as college students.

"I know, but I'm just saying. I could get double the amount
for this price." Somehow, I'm still stuck in Asia-pricing, which
doesn't make sense because it's been over a month since I
returned to the United States. Maybe I just have an underlying

problem of excessive stinginess. Amanda and I both laugh at how ridiculous I sound.

"Some things never change," she says.

After reaching the front of the line, we order our drinks and find a table towards the center of the small shop. Our awaited boba is only a moment away. Amanda starts updating me on her life. The gym has become her second home, making regular trips five days a week. In addition, she has been meticulously building an E-Sports community at Hendrix College by hosting tournaments, all while hoping to start her own fashion line. Once a shy and quiet girl, Amanda now brims with confidence.

"Taro slush and Thai tea with boba!"

"That's us Kenny," Amanda says.

I settle back in my seat, handing Amanda her Taro slush. I start to shake the contents in my cup when the conversation shifts to me.

"So how was your big Asia trip?" she asks.

I spent the first month and a half of this past summer visiting various countries in Southeast and East Asia. I start to tell Amanda stories about my late night escapades in Hong Kong, the time I ate the best Pad Thai in Bangkok, and how I visited some of the filming locations from *Crazy Rich Asians* in Singapore. Then I talk about Siem Reap. "You know in

Cambodia, our tour guide helped us buy fried crickets from these street vendors, and he said they went well with beer... I never got to try that, but by themselves they were still good!"

Amanda's eyes light up. "You know, I showed my parents your Facebook posts from Cambodia, and they loved them. They haven't been back since they moved to Arkansas."

"Can I ask? Did they have to escape from the Khmer Rouge? Is that why y'all are here?"

Amanda pauses. She takes a sip of taro slush before answering. "Yeah, both of my parents lived through it, but I think they were lucky. My parents talk about Cambodia all the time, especially my dad."

Siem Reap, Cambodia was a unique experience in contrast to my other travels. I was there in the middle of June for three days before flying to Hong Kong. I initially arrived in Siem Reap expecting a typical tourist experience similar to the other places I visited that summer, and to some extent, I did. I tried new food, visited ancient monuments, and soaked in the local culture. It was not until departing when I reflected upon my interactions with the people in Siem Reap that I realized how influential the country's history had been in shaping my experience there. Awareness of Cambodia's war-ravaged past, specifically the infamous Cambodian Genocide committed by the Khmer Rouge, was saddening. It wasn't the kind of feeling someone on vacation expects.

It was our second day in Siem Reap, and I remembered our tour guide Mitt bidding us farewell from his van. As he drove away, my friends and I walked to a seemingly reputable looking Cambodian barbeque place on Pub Street, not too far from our hostel. After we ordered a meat platter, a waiter brought us a small grill and burner. The grill had a mound in the center where the meat cooked, and a moat around the perimeter for the soup to boil. Shortly afterwards, the raw meat platter arrived with a plate of vegetables and steaming white rice. Exhausted from a morning's exploration of ancient temples at Angkor Wat, I devoured my first round of food.

As I waited for more meat to cook, I turned my head towards the street to people-watch. Like the clubs, most restaurants on Pub Street were outdoor with roof awnings. A few tables away, sitting close to the entrance, were two white Western tourists who were suddenly approached by children likely asking for money—I only assumed since that had been my experience with Cambodian children on Pub Street so far. I observed as they started playing with them as if they were their own, even putting them on their laps. It may have been just me, but the affection seemed a bit odd. They aren't stray animals asking to be petted, I thought. The kids finally left after they received a few dollars.

Next, an armless Khmer man approached them. He wore a basket around his neck filled with books. The two Western men took a second to look at his collection before waving him off signaling they were not interested. The armless salesman made eye contact with me and walked over to our table. He gestured for us to take a slip of paper from his basket explaining that he was an army veteran selling books to make a quiet living for himself. The paper also said he had lost both of his arms from landmines. Out of courtesy, we checked his collection of books which took up the rest of the space in his basket. One caught my eye, and I picked it up.

Children of Cambodia's Killing Fields by Dith Pran. Upon further examination, the book was a collection of memoirs written by people who grew up as children during the era of the Khmer Rouge. I've heard of the name, the Khmer Rouge, and I knew they caused the worst genocide in modern Cambodian history, but the details of what happened remained unknown to me.

"I'll take this one," I told him.

He gave me a price, and after some haggling, he motioned with the nubs of his arms toward his right pocket where I placed the money. After he left, I looked down at my new purchase with anticipation. What better way to learn history than to read the voices who witnessed it?

My friends and I retreated to the hostel to take a midday nap, drained from the day's events. They all dove into their beds and immediately passed out while I sat in mine, still clutching my new book. Instead of falling asleep, I opened to the first page and became immersed in a continuous cycle of despair. It all seemed the same: starvation, disease, forced labor, senseless murder, soldiers brainwashed with corrupted communist ideology, and of course... despair. It was genocide, except in my mind, it became more than a dictionary definition. Eventually my eyes stopped watering as the accounts slowly desensitized me, followed by a wave of frustration. I came into the country blind, preoccupied with taking the best pictures for social media, yet I hadn't even bothered to research beforehand the history of suffering the people here had endured.

We had no plans for our final day in Siem Reap. Still reeling from those child memoirs, I asked my friends if we could visit a few museums. They agreed and we all pulled out our phones to start searching nearby. Not too far from our hostel, we found a local *tuk tuk* driver parked on the side of the dirt road. One of my friends approached the man and pointed to the addresses he found on his phone screen. "How much is it if you take us to these places?" he asked. The driver offered us a deal where he would take us to a war museum and then Wat Thmei, the memorial of the Siem Reap killing fields. After a thirty-minute drive, we arrived at our first stop, the war museum. Our driver told us he would wait for us to finish and pointed us towards the ticket-booth entrance.

We entered inside onto a grassy field filled with tanks and military machinery. To the side were message boards under a wooden colonnade that displayed facts about Cambodia's wars and military conflicts. Adjacent to the boards and on the walls were rifles and knives. A worker from the museum approached us and said we could request a free English tour of the museum, to which we all agreed.

Shortly afterwards, an older Khmer man approached us and introduced himself as Cat. He explained that his nickname came from his fellow soldiers who witnessed him survive many near-death experiences, and they all said he had "nine lives" just like a cat. Cat gave us a description of all the weapons and vehicles in the museum. I learned that the war machines on display either came from the United States, China, or the Soviet Union, a symbol of how influential these superpowers were during the Cold War, and specifically the armed conflicts in Cambodia. Cat then took us to the colonnade where the firearms were on display, and he showed us some of the rifles Cambodia used during its three decades of conflict. He even let us hold an AK-47.

As Cat provided history on military firearms, I read the message boards that compiled written Cambodian war history with corresponding photographs. I skimmed through the text because the tour was moving fast, and since I was clueless about most of Cambodian history, my attention mainly focused on the sections about the Khmer Rouge.

At the end of the tour, Cat started talking about landmines. Decades of war resulted in Cambodia today being one of the most heavily mined countries in the world. Even though the fighting has stopped, Cambodians today were still being injured or killed by hidden landmines and unexploded devices. As tourists, we were heavily discouraged from exploring remote locations without guidance from local authorities. Cat lifted his right pant leg to reveal a metal prosthetic. He explained that he lost his right leg from a landmine while serving in the army, reminding me of the armless bookseller the day before who had faced a similar fate. To emphasize Cambodia's ongoing landmine problem, Cat took out his smartphone and showed us a picture of a landmine completely uncovered on the grass. It could have been mistaken for a rusty cast-iron pot.

"My neighbor found this in his backyard a few weeks ago," he said.

We tipped Cat a few dollars each and thanked him for sharing his experiences with us. We lingered a little longer before returning to our *tuk tuk* driver who took us to our second and final stop in Wat Thmei, the memorial of the Siem Reap killing fields.

The term "killing fields" was not familiar to me until I started to read those memoirs. When the Khmer Rouge were in control of Cambodia from 1975-1979, they starved and executed millions of people in villages that were run like slave labor camps. They placed the dead in mass graves, usually in the wilderness outside of these villages, thus earning the infamous term "killing fields."

When I entered the memorial, I learned even more information about the Khmer Rouge, and I wondered how this country had endured so much pain. The people I met over the time I spent in Siem Reap all seemed at peace with their lives. It may be hard to erase that trauma, but at least it seemed like the people were healing. I left Cambodia later that night, with the harsh, disturbing reality of the Khmer Rouge imprinted in my mind.

Amanda and I keep discussing the Khmer Rouge, and how it affected her family. After sharing my experiences in Siem Reap with her, I learned that her father, Mr. Lee, along with his wife, owns a small Chinese takeout restaurant called Oriental Kitchen. I'm surprised I have never heard of it before as I thought I knew all the Asian spots in our small college town. The conversation soon returned to Mr. Lee's life under the Khmer Rouge.

"My dad can get really annoying sometimes because of how much he talks about it. He mentions wanting some written documentation about his past, but he's never done it. I think running the restaurant makes him too busy to think about it."

I sip my drink for a second, and suddenly, an idea emerges.

"For my honors minor I have to do a capstone project before I graduate, and I've been thinking about writing a book."

"So?"

"So… What if I write his story for him?"

"Are you serious? I think he would love that!" Amanda says.

After finishing our drinks, I tell Amanda to meet me at my dorm. As soon as I arrive, I search my bedside drawer for Dith Pran's book. "Whether or not we write this book, I think you and your family would like this," I say, as I hand it over to Amanda.

Amanda smiles, then tells me she has to leave.

"Thank you for tonight. I'll keep you updated."

Two weeks later, the dashboard of my gray Honda Civic reads 5:30 p.m. as I park in front of a white brick building. Adjacent to it is the gas station on the corner of Prince Street and Morningside Drive that Amanda had described. Yellow letters in a glass window next to the door read:

Welcome to the Oriental Kitchen:
Serving Healthy, Fresh, and Delicious Food
Daily Since 1985

Amanda meets me at a screen door at the back of the restaurant and ushers me inside the kitchen. I hear the chop of a knife on a cutting board as I turn my head towards the sound. In the middle of the room sits a dark-haired woman atop a stool wearing a white apron.

"Kenny, this is my mom."

She stops me by raising her gloved hands, covered in raw meat, signaling that I probably should not shake them. Then she smiles at me, revealing the dimples in her cheeks. I laugh awkwardly and wave to say hello as a greeting. Without hesitation, Mrs. Lee fires question after question about myself, my trip to Siem Reap, and the book I want to write about her husband. She tells me about her childhood growing up in her village in Cambodia. She recounts how she heard the American bombs and how the people in her village were brainwashed by the propaganda put forth by the Khmer Rouge. As we talk for several minutes, Mrs. Lee has forgotten about her work and has instead turned her entire focus to me. I thought Amanda said her father was the talkative one. Her mother may rival him.

"Amanda, give him some water," Mrs. Lee says.

Amanda walks over to a shelf supporting all of the restaurant's styrofoam cups, takeout boxes, paper oyster pails, and plastic bags. She grabs a cup and heads towards the sink behind me. After glancing at the clock, Mrs. Lee tells me she needs to continue working. Amanda hands me my water and leads me past the front door of the kitchen.

There are two sets of booths in the corner of the room, the only sitting area for customers. Amanda and I pick the booth farthest from the kitchen and sit facing each other. The wall dividing the kitchen from the dining area has an open rectangular frame with a bell on the counter. Underneath the frame are paper pamphlets kept in built-in wooden pockets, likely their takeout menu. I make a mental note to grab one before I leave.

An hour has passed and Mr. Lee still has not arrived.

"Sorry about this. He's not the most punctual person sometimes," Amanda assures me after my eyes dart towards my watch. "He's still at the store. He's been running errands all day."

"Don't worry, really, it's fine," I say. I can't hold a grudge at someone for not showing up on time as I am not the most punctual person myself.

A few minutes later, I hear the back door in the kitchen open. Then I hear the voice of a man talking to Mrs. Lee in what sounds like a Chinese dialect. After a brief conversation, the sound of flip-flops approaches the door to the kitchen. I immediately stand up.

"You must be Kenny, nice to meet you. I am Amanda's father," the man says. He reaches out his hand, and I hasten to shake it. Mr. Lee is an older man wearing an oversized gray T-shirt, a pair of gym shorts, and the Nike slides on his feet explained the flip-flop noise from earlier. His hair is short and spiked up, colored in a coat of light gray.

"I had to stop by Sam's Club to buy some ingredients," he says. Mr. Lee grabs a gray, metal folding chair from the corner of the room and places it against the wall so he can face me.

Why he doesn't sit in the opposite booth is unbeknownst to me as Amanda has since retreated to the kitchen.

"Thank you Mr. Lee for meeting with me. I'm sure Amanda has told you about how I want to help write your story."

"Yes, she told me a lot. It intrigued me."

The more I explain myself, the more my internal unease mounts. Why am I here? I don't know how to conduct an interview. I don't even have a list of questions for him. Where do I start? I hadn't done any prior research outside of what I faintly remember from my trip almost two months ago. Is this selfish? Should I do this project?

The air is heavy with tension; Mr. Lee can probably read my apprehension. Right now though, I have to act. I need to start somewhere. I pull out my iPhone and open to voice memos.

"Do you mind if I record our conversation? I'm gonna use the audio later to transcribe what you will say into words," I say.

"Yeah, it makes sense."

I press a red circle at the bottom of the screen. My cellphone is now an audio recorder.

"Ok... So, what do you remember about Cambodia before the Khmer Rouge?"

CHILDHOOD IN PHNOM PENH

M R. LEE WAS born in 1961 in Cambodia's capital Phnom Penh to immigrant parents from the Guangdong Province in China. Mr. Lee's father, Dak, came from a wealthy business family, and after marrying, moved his family to Saigon to help with the family business there. According to Mr. Lee, to put into scale how wealthy Dak's family was, their business owned one of two telephones in all of Saigon. While in Vietnam, Dak and his wife Guang had their first five children: the eldest daughter Gia, followed by Chang, Teng, Heng and Bieng. They lived comfortably in Saigon for some time until Dak moved his family again to Phnom Penh where his brother Seng, Mr. Lee, and their youngest child, Guah, was born. In total, the Lee family had ten members with Mr. Lee being the second youngest of eight siblings.

Growing up in a predominantly Chinese district in Phnom Penh, Mr. Lee saw signs in Khmer, but heard Mandarin spoken in the streets. He spoke Teochew at home and attended a Chinese school where he also learned Mandarin. Despite being born in Cambodia's capital city, he couldn't speak Khmer.

Mr. Lee lived on the second floor of a four-story housing complex. The Lees lived at the very front, in a one-room apartment the size of a master's bedroom. The unit also came with a ladder giving access to a small attic and balcony overlooking the local market.

With such limited space, and with Dak as the only source of income for ten people, there were few furnishings. There was a queen-sized bed tucked in one corner where Guang, Dak, Mr. Lee, and Guah would sleep. During the day there was a desk and chairs that served as the dining room table and a study area for the kids. At night, Teng, Gia and Heng would team up to stack the chairs and push the table to the corner to make space for a colorful sedge mat on the floor where the three of them would sleep. The younger children, Seng, Chang and Bieng, were on a separate mat in the attic. There was also a wooden chest that the family used as a sofa as well as storage space.

Mr. Lee describes life on the second floor as cramped but never uncomfortable. There was a set of stairs serving as the only entrance and exit between the four floors located at the back of the building. Upon entering the second floor from the back staircase, there was a narrow hallway lined by four screen doors, three of which were also one-room apartments that each housed seven to ten people. The fourth room closest to the staircase contained a shared kitchen, toilet, and shower. The Lees lived at the end of the hallway. Throughout the day, the floor was practically empty except for small children, housewives, and the elderly. Dak would be at work, and the older children were at school. Nighttime, however, was a different story altogether.

A shared kitchen and bathroom in an already tight housing complex was a recipe for disaster in terms of congestion and a lack of privacy. Since the toilet and shower were located in the same area as the kitchen, it became incredibly cramped during mealtimes. However, it was at its worst at night because that was when everyone from school or work came home. Sometimes lines to use the shower and the bathroom would be so long that people had to wait inside other families' units to lessen the number of people in the hallway. Even though privacy was nonexistent, nobody ever seemed to mind. Rarely was there any fighting, and if there was, it was amongst the younger kids. Patience was necessary to learn. To Mr. Lee, everyone considered each other family.

Over 40 years later in a Los Angeles hotel room, Dak and half of his children including Mr. Lee reunited to mourn over the loss of Guang who had died a few hours earlier due to complications from her old age. As he poured his 4th glass of whiskey, Dak recounted how he met and fell in love with Guang. "She was very beautiful, but I paid attention not because of her looks, but because she had a beautiful heart," he said.

When Dak was young and starting out in his professional career, his parents pushed him to marry, and they worked tirelessly to set him up with young, beautiful women from his hometown. Dak may have had up to 15 first dates although few led to a second one. They all seemed uninspiring to Dak, who admitted he forgot most of their names the next morning. It wasn't until he met Guang that everything changed for him.

Guang, who was touted as one of the most beautiful women in the town, was also one of the nicest people you would ever meet. In Saigon, she still wore traditional Chinese silk dresses as opposed to typical Vietnamese street clothes because they were the only garments she had. Every time Guang was out in the market buying groceries, she was often met with malicious and jealous stares from the Vietnamese locals. Some mocked her clothes, and others threw rocks at her. It seemed tasteless at the time to wear such nice clothes at a local market. Despite the abuse, Guang never retaliated; in fact, she always had a smile on her face.

In Cambodia, Guang maintained her same role as a housewife, working tirelessly at all hours of the day. Mr. Lee would hardly see his mother stop moving to read the newspaper or take a break. She was always doing a chore to keep busy. Since the family had neither the money nor space for a refrigerator, Guang bought groceries every day from the market across the street. She kept the house clean and cooked all of the meals for the family. According to Mr. Lee, Guang was a "damn good" cook. It wasn't fancy food like lobster or shrimp, but simple classics like stir-fried vegetables with pork and rice, sweet and sour fish soup, steamed rice that looked and tasted like fried rice, and various noodle dishes. When she felt like spoiling the family, she would boil chopped pieces of taro root.

Everyone on the second floor loved Guang. She wasn't just the mother to her own family but to everyone, especially the little children on the floor who called her "mama." While the neighbors were away, she would often babysit those too young to go to school. Guang was always ready to clean up a child dirty from defecating or playing outside. The neighbors also gave Guang a small budget to pay for food, so she occasionally cooked for them as well.

Guang was always thinking about other people, not just her family. There would be days after school when Mr. Lee would wait for his mother to return from the market knowing she had promised him his favorite snacks, only to be disappointed when she came back empty-handed.

"You didn't bring me any snacks?" Mr. Lee demanded.

"I did… but I saw some of the neighbor's kids on the street, and I had to give them some because they begged for a snack," Guang said with a guilty face.

"Mom, I'm your son!"

Guang would merely smile and say. "It's alright, I'll bring you some tomorrow."

When Guang did provide Mr. Lee with his favorite snacks, she expected him to always be generous. One day, she watched as a 7-year-old Mr. Lee split his rice cake in two to share with his friend. One piece came out to be much smaller and looked less appealing, so he offered that piece to his friend. Guang who saw this exchange stopped and scolded Mr. Lee.

"When you want to share something with someone, you give them the best option. When you decide to give or sacrifice something for somebody, it means that you love them. Love is not love until you give it away," she said. These words resonated with Mr. Lee when opportunities arose for him to be generous.

Mr. Lee would sometimes accompany Guang to the market where he watched as his mother's personality was on full display. She was always so warm and friendly, even to people she didn't know. When examining fresh fish with a stranger, Guang would always smile and prompt conversation. She had a charm that made people feel comfortable around her. Mr. Lee sometimes had to remind Guang she still had chores at home, because she would lose track of time talking and laughing with anyone who would listen.

There would be other times, mainly when he was younger, when Mr. Lee would go with Guang to visit relatives. They took a form of public transportation called cyclos, which were easy to find as they were usually parked by street curbs right outside the market. Cyclos were tricycle rickshaws that looked almost like wheelchairs except there would be a cyclist behind the chair where Mr. Lee and Guang sat. Once they reached their destination, Guang always tipped the cyclist even though tipping in Phnom Penh back then was uncommon. Mr. Lee remembered seeing the expressions of gratitude on their faces usually followed by a bow and a "sister you are so kind."

Guang was even more selfless to Dak's family than he was himself. One night, while the family was having dinner, they received a knock at the door. The door opened to Uncle Chen, Dak's youngest brother. He had escaped to Cambodia to avoid the draft in Vietnam, and his parents told him to find Dak at his address in Phnom Penh. Uncle Chen was looking for a place to live until the war calmed down. Dak, who was hesitant to let him stay, was ignored by Guang who immediately accepted his request.

"We already have ten mouths to feed and eight children going to school," Dak argued.

"He came all the way from Vietnam to look for you, for your help, and you're not going to because it's inconvenient?" Guang retorted.

Dak conceded and Uncle Chen was part of the family for a few years. Mr. Lee believes he boasts about Guang every time he mentions her, but it's because that is how he sees his mother: a superhero.

Mr. Lee remembers life in 1960s Phnom Penh as laid back. Crime was low, the streets were clean, and the roads were rarely jammed with traffic. It was a mid-sized, budding capital city with a population of no more than 600,000 people. Dak worked a white-collar job on the same block of the house for an export company. He was also an interpreter for them because he was well versed in 6 languages including Vietnamese, French, and Lao. His office was on the first floor of his boss's house, whose family lived upstairs. Mr. Lee occasionally walked past his dad's work and observed from a distance to avoid detection. Dak was usually on the phone, in a meeting, or reading a newspaper. His favorite hobby was listening to BBC on the radio at home because he liked to stay up to date on current events. By 1973, Dak had fully engrossed himself with updates on the Cambodian Civil War. Ever since the ousting of Prince Sihanouk by Prime Minister Lon Nol and Prince Sirik Matak's military coup three years earlier, violence in the Khmer Republic had escalated. In Phnom Penh, the effects of violence had not yet been felt. However, the *riel* began to inflate, and financially the Lee family struggled to make ends meet.

At this same time Gia—Mr. Lee's oldest sister—was a nurse who trained and worked under Aunt Ain, a physician who ran her own maternity clinic. She used to be a teacher who left to go north at the border after graduating high school. However, as the Civil War intensified, Gia, desperate for money, sought help from Aunt Ain. After accepting the job, Gia would only visit the family once or twice a week because she was provided a bedroom at the clinic. Meanwhile, Heng had moved to Macau for school, and Uncle Chen had moved back to Saigon.

Ever since Heng left, Chang moved downstairs to sleep which meant Mr. Lee relocated to the attic. It wasn't any more peaceful than sleeping downstairs because he could still hear every conversation downstairs. Mr. Lee was preparing for bed one night when he heard his parents arguing.

"I'm moving back to Saigon. My family found work for me," Dak said.

"I don't understand," Guang said.

"Like I said. I lost my job, and we need the money."

Nobody else was in the room except Seng, who was also in the attic. The news broke the next morning to everyone's dismay, but they all understood it was the best decision. In the meantime, Dak began detailing proper precautions should danger arise.

"In the future, if anything happens, they will probably evacuate everyone. Make sure you all stick together. If anyone is separated, remember we all have a birthmark on our right arms. Look for that birthmark," Dak said. "If you can't find anyone in our family, stick with the person closest to you... whether it be our neighbors, a close relative, or a friend you meet along the way. At the very least, stick to somebody you know."

Mr. Lee pauses the story. He has been crossing his left foot over his right knee in his chair, sometimes looking up at the ceiling as he talks. He's been doing it a lot every time he finds himself in deep thought. Then, the tone in his voice is awestruck as he continues talking.

"Man, I recalled that he said that, predicting that we could have been separated, and that we could use our birthmarks to identify each other. Man... that was just awesome." At the age of 12, Mr. Lee was too young to comprehend what his father said that day, but the coming years awoke Mr. Lee to the nightmarish reality of that statement.

The Chinese school Mr. Lee attended had shut down, which meant that Gia was the only sibling to graduate high school. In an effort to keep her children productive, Guang insisted they help the household make money or continue to self-educate.

Teng did both. He found a job and worked by day, and at night he, along with Bieng, took private tutoring lessons in English. Chang would also get involved in this new tutoring economy by helping with Mandarin privately at households. Seng worked as an errand boy for a currency exchange company, and Mr. Lee would sometimes see him riding around on a company bike. At night when he would come home, they would always play together. This left Mr. Lee and Guah, who were still too young to work a formal job.

"My mom gave me a chicken box…about…" Mr. Lee leaves his chair to bend down and draw an imaginary rectangle on the floor with his fingers. "I think it was about 18x30 inches. I used this box to sell candy at the central market in our area."

Mr. Lee would take his youngest sister and sit on the sidewalk right outside the market with the chicken box full of candy. Over the next few months, the streets started to crowd with displaced people from the rural villages who were forced to flee from the war. Most lined the streets because they were homeless and looking for shelter, but some started competing with Mr. Lee by setting up their own tables and becoming street vendors themselves. Mr. Lee also started noticing Lon Nol's soldiers bullying the street vendors around.

"They could kick you like a ball, they don't care. They came back from war and became very wild."

Mr. Lee would constantly see soldiers harass vendors for things like free cigarettes. Sometimes they even demanded cash.

Due to internal displacement after Lon Nol took power, Phnom Penh's population had swelled from 600,000 to 2

million people. As years passed, the Civil War continued, and the Khmer Rouge along with the other revolutionaries under Sihanouk's FUNK were gaining more territory. The more of the country they captured, the more they inched towards the capital. Around the start of 1975, Mr. Lee, who was almost 14 years old, began to hear bombs. At first, they were distant, but over time the noises grew louder. Everyone in the capital was on edge.

It was April 8, 1975.

"I'm leaving to go to the market, are you coming?" It was early in the morning, and Guang was about to head to the market with Guah. As Mr. Lee had gotten older, he had stopped accompanying his mother because he wanted to sleep as much as possible before school. Now that school was closed, he had started going with her again.

"I don't feel like it today," Mr. Lee replied.

Mr. Lee was usually full of energy, but that day was different. That day he was weary. Perhaps noticing his demeanor, Guang advised him to, "eat breakfast, wash up, and go play with your friends."

There was an alley near the apartments where many of his friends from the neighborhood and Seng would play every morning. Most of the kids did not own toys, so they resorted to playing with whatever they could find. Mr. Lee's favorite game was one where he pretended to be a soldier. He would pull a rubber band from his thumb like a slingshot, and he would flick wadded-up paper or bottle caps at the other kids. When Gia was still in high school, she would carry Mr. Lee on her shoulders to the alley where she would watch him and Seng play with the others; Mr. Lee would even refer to her as his "second mama."

The early-morning sun was out which was the perfect time to play because it wasn't too hot. However, he wasn't sure why, but today he hesitated going to the alley.

Mr. Lee had been sitting and eating at the dining table when all of a sudden, he heard the whizz of a rocket-bomb coming from a distance. Mr. Lee had been conditioned to hearing the rockets in the air; however, this one felt eerily different. The sound of the rocket grew louder. The whizzing now sounded like an old turbine turning, a *cluk cluk cluk* sound. In an instant, Mr. Lee's worst fears were realized as the bomb exploded within earshot.

There was a loud boom which made the whole house shake and the walls reverberate. Mr. Lee dashed out of the building to chaos in the streets. Everyone of all ages was in a panic; children, adults, men and women alike were confused, running, and wailing. Mr. Lee noticed a cloud of black smoke and headed towards it. His heart raced and stomach dropped when he realized his feet were running down an all-too familiar path. Mr. Lee arrived at the alley and froze, immobilized at the huge hole in the wall. Shrapnel from the blast resulted in massive collateral damage to the surrounding buildings and streets, but the wreckage was nothing compared to the sight of his playmates lying about in various stages of mutilation.

One girl was struggling to stand as she held the huge gash—probably from shrapnel—on her right breast, almost like she was sliced by a samurai sword. Blood flowed from her gash, but she wasn't crying. Her face was stoic. Another boy he usually played with was dead; the hole in his lungs indicating that he was killed instantly. Not too far from the corpse was the dead boy's younger brother who was missing his left leg. He left a trail of blood behind him as he struggled to crawl away from the rubble. Mr. Lee was petrified, bewildered, and shocked at the scene before him. Eventually, the parents of the two boys arrived at the scene, and upon seeing what was left of their sons, the father immediately fainted while their mother simply stood paralyzed, trying to hold it together. The son with the missing leg crawled into her arms. Thankfully, he managed to survive.

When the police finally appeared, Mr. Lee ran back home. Guang's face was wet with tears, and her eyes were reddened.

She saw her son and tightly embraced him. They both knew that the war was inching closer to Phnom Penh. Everyone in the city did.

EVACUATION

EIGHT DAYS AFTER the alley bombing, Gia told the family she again had to work overtime.

"But you promised," Guang objected.

Tomorrow was the start of the Cambodian New Year, and Guang wanted the whole family home together to celebrate. Ever since the bombs reached Phnom Penh, many workers from the clinic started resigning. In fact, as the war progressed, doctors and a number of medical personnel fled to France or other western countries. The city's rapid population growth strained the already understaffed medical facilities; they were overcrowded and often unsanitary with an acute shortage of medicine and equipment.

"I promise. I will try and be home by tonight," Gia said.

Her co-worker who lived next door came inside.

"Gia, let's go."

Gia waved at her family. "Have a good day everyone," she said. Her co-worker was holding the door open waiting, and together they left for work. Mr. Lee never realized Gia's wave would be her last.

Throughout the day, Mr. Lee heard gunshots and artillery fire inching closer and closer. Lon Nol's defenses were being pushed to their limit. The fighting continued throughout the night making it difficult for Mr. Lee to fall asleep. Concern for Gia pervaded his thoughts, making sleep impossible. When will she come home? Was she still alive?

Before he realized it, dawn was approaching. The first rays of sunlight welcoming the New Year started to penetrate the windows and shine through the cracks in the attic floor. Restless, Mr. Lee crept downstairs to the balcony. He watched as the sun slowly rose. Maybe, he thought, Gia would appear, exhausted, yearning for a quick shower and some sleep. However, she never came. Instead, a black Mercedes Benz stopped in the middle of the road right in front of his view. Two soldiers came out of the car. They looked to be about 16-17 years old, and they were speaking Khmer. The best Mr. Lee could do at the time was interpret what they were saying. He couldn't speak Khmer, but he could understand bits of it.

The soldiers were yelling at the driver to get out of the car. The driver stayed, still seated in the car. He stubbornly told the two teenage soldiers he was just the driver, and that his job was to drive them to their destination.

"I told you to get out of the car right now!" one of the soldiers yelled.

This time the driver did not resist. He looked about 35-40 years old. His appearance was unkempt and his hair graying. His face was tired, probably from the stress of the prior weeks. The teen soldier that yelled looked back at the driver who was cowering in fear. Without saying another word, he pointed his rifle at the driver and fired two shots into his head. The unkempt driver dropped to the ground. His body lay limp as a pool of blood started to form. Instead of watching the start of a new day, Mr. Lee witnessed the end of someone's life. It would not be the last time.

Mr. Lee was on his knees. Hopefully, the soldiers wouldn't notice him. His heart raced, and he started to perspire. For the first time in his short life, Mr. Lee feared death. From inside the room, Guang whispered for him to come back inside. Mr. Lee crawled to his mother's voice.

"Mother, someone got killed," Mr. Lee said.

"Be quiet. Don't make any noise," she said. The rest of his siblings had formed a huddle with her in the living room. Mr. Lee joined them and together waited in silence for something to happen. As the sun rose, they heard an army marching in with vehicles. Suddenly, men were shouting from their megaphones.

"Everyone must leave! The Americans are going to bomb the city!"

Soldiers stormed the housing complex hollering the same message at residents. When they reached the Lees, everyone in the house scrambled to grab important belongings. Instead of packing, Mr. Lee went to the balcony to check out the commotion. He looked down and saw the driver's body missing, replaced with armed green-uniformed soldiers and military trucks. They were still yelling out instructions.

"Everyone calm down! It is the start of the New Year! We will celebrate for the next three days!"

Mr. Lee was excited when he heard the word celebrate, and without thinking, he dashed down the stairs while his family was frantically packing. Before he knew it, he was on the street. He observed as people joyfully climbed onto the backs of military trucks. Thinking it was part of the celebration, Mr. Lee followed suit.

The truck he embarked on started moving, and as it passed by other nearby areas in the city, Mr. Lee saw families welcoming the incoming soldiers by waving white flags. Other households draped white flags fashioned from bed sheets on windows and rooftops. The truck passed by a scene where soldiers were firing shots at innocent people on the second-floor balcony of an apartment building. The scene suddenly felt predatory. Mr. Lee soon realized that this was not a peaceful New Year's celebration, and when the truck stopped, he scrambled out and ran back home.

"Where have you been?" Guang demanded.

She didn't receive a response. Mr. Lee, who was normally a noisy and outspoken teenager, was silent, like he had seen a ghost.

There was no time to catch up because the soldiers were getting impatient. They started firing their rifles in the air as a scare tactic to rush everyone out.

"The Americans are going to bomb the city! Everyone must leave!"

Guang told the family to stay close to her. She handed everyone a plastic bag of clothes, snacks, and water. Guang's bag carried a mosquito net and some gold from her jewelry collection. Mr. Lee stayed attached to his mother and his remaining 5 siblings as they followed their second-floor neighbors outside.

Out on the street, more people were congregating, and the crowd grew. Some were already telling Guang that the invading soldiers were already shooting at whomever they pleased. They were also rounding up professionals, teachers, and government workers.

Eventually, the crowd was led to a bridge and was joined with the hundreds of other Cambodians. Mr. Lee observed as children ran around crying out for their parents. He looked over at a pregnant woman lying on the ground nearby and breathing heavily with blood coming out from her uterus. Her body was losing color and it looked like she was slowly dying. Nobody around her cared enough to be concerned. People thought of nothing but their own survival.

Armed soldiers guarded the group on all sides of the bridge, locking refugees in like animals in a slaughterhouse. Mr. Lee asked around and was told that Lon Nol lost, and that the soldiers were the Khmer Rouge and their supporting cadres. However, those not directly associated with the Khmer Rouge were quickly exterminated, signaling that even the slightest deviation from the ruling party was prohibited.

Fidgeting in his metal chair, Mr. Lee pauses for a moment.

"Starting on that day, we all lost our freedom," he says.

The Khmer Rouge soldiers led everyone to a vast market area which would act as a stopover for the next few days. Mr. Lee's group was met with another crowd who had already been at the market for some time. As soon as everyone settled in, people, including Mr. Lee started asking around for news. One man told him that in three days the Khmer Rouge would lead everyone back to their homes after the American bombs passed. He seemed optimistic. It was starting to get dark, so Mr. Lee headed back to his family under the illusion that things would start looking up.

Guang had laid out a thin blanket separating the 7 of them from the dirt. As everyone laid down, she covered them with the mosquito net. Their neighbors from the apartment had set up camps nearby.

The next day brought more waiting. People were becoming tense as there was a lack of transparency from the soldiers who refused to provide any more information about the current situation. Instead, they were tying people's arms behind their backs and shooting machine guns in the air as a scare tactic. By the third day, it became clear the Khmer Rouge had no intent to return them to their homes. Two out of the three families that had lived alongside the Lees on the second floor had now fled to the countryside seeking refuge with relatives living there.

The remaining family next to them were the last of their neighbors. They had a two-year-old daughter battling a high fever since arriving at the market. The girl looked dehydrated, and the family had no water. Guang, who had always babysat her, stayed by her side until she suddenly took a turn for the worst.

Immediately, Guang rushed to find the girl something to drink. Mr. Lee watched helplessly from his blanket as the girl was so consumed with agony she refused even the loving touch of her own mother. Not too long after Guang left, her eyes slowly started to close, and Mr. Lee watched her breathe her last breath.

The next few days at the market were miserable. There was no bathroom, medicine, or clean water, and the market was starting to run out of food. Everyone slept on the dirt unless they were prepared like the Lees with a tarp or a blanket. One day it rained, wet clothing and muddy feet heightening the overall feelings of despair. The sounds of traffic and everyday city life were replaced by sobs and cries of anguish. Finally, the soldiers decided it was time to start moving, forcing everyone to walk southeast along Highway One, away from the city.

To realize his agrarian utopia, Pol Pot and other Khmer Rouge leaders first facilitated the mass migration of citizens in cities like Phnom Penh to rural villages across the country so that every citizen could work as a farmer. Currently, Mr. Lee and the remaining seven members of his family had been on the move for what seemed about a week. The crowd moved as one, shuffling their way along the highway like animals corralled into the stocks. The longer Mr. Lee walked, the more people he saw die.

"Pol Pot's soldiers only cared if you kept moving. If you slow down, they don't discriminate. They will shoot you: sick, handicap, old, young, it don't matter, you had to move." Mr. Lee says, shaking his head in disbelief before continuing to talk in a frustrated tone.

The job of these soldiers was to escort those strong enough to endure without food, water, or medical attention, ignoring those who were dying of starvation. Guang's resourcefulness kept the family somewhat fed. Using her experience shopping at the local market every day, she found plants she thought were edible. Sometimes she dug into the ground to find wild potatoes. It made Mr. Lee and his other siblings sick, but it wasn't enough to kill them. Others weren't as lucky as they ate plants that were too poisonous.

The only time people had a chance to eat real food was when they passed neighboring villages already seized and indoctrinated by the Khmer Rouge. The villages acted like rest stops where the inhabitants offered goods in exchange for gold, as paper currency had become worthless. However, such exchanges were near impossible for ordinary citizens.

"They offered us rice and salt in exchange for jewelry… 30 pounds of rice for an ounce of gold. Who the hell has that much gold?" Mr. Lee says.

Finally, the Lee family followed their group to a village approximately 40 km from Phnom Penh. The area was desolate and damaged from all the bombs. The Khmer Rouge soldiers told everyone to record how many people were in their families. Then, after inspection, families were told to construct their own shelters as a way to help rebuild the village.

"That village was the worst hell I've ever experienced in my life. But I'll tell you that story the next time you come back," Mr. Lee says. He ends the interview with that statement and asks what I think. I look at my wristwatch and see two hours have passed since the interview started. Since it is still summer, there is still daylight outside even though it's past eight. I think about an answer to his question, but I am unsure what to tell him.

"I look forward to writing the rest of your story," I say as I reach out and cordially shake his hand. Both of us walk back into the kitchen where Amanda and her mother have waited the whole time.

Amanda is sitting on a wooden stool eating the dinner her mother prepared. Mrs. Lee is still chopping up chicken breast. As Mr. Lee and I walk in, Mrs. Lee looks up from her work.

"Do you like chicken feet? I made extra for you. Eat it as a snack."

Little does she know how I devoured chicken feet in Asia.

"Yes! I love chicken feet!"

Mrs. Lee leaves her seat, grabs a to-go box, fills it to the brim with steaming hot white rice, and another to-go box of chicken feet. Now my face starts to flush.

"Please, this is too much. Let me pay for this," I say.

Mrs. Lee ignores my plea and hands me the food wrapped up in a plastic bag. All I could do is half-heartedly smile.

"Don't worry about it," she says.

As I turn to leave, I look back at Amanda who is still eating. She smiles and shrugs her shoulders.

"You know this. It's Asian hospitality."

PART 2
EVIL'S WORLD

VAMPIRE MOSQUITOS

MR. LEE AND I have agreed to meet every other Sunday night since those are the days his restaurant is closed for the entire day. Two Sundays later, I find the gas station, turn into Morningside Drive, and find the white bricks of the small takeout restaurant tucked away towards the back. As I park in the same spot in front of the entrance, Amanda is already there waiting. When she sees my car, she waves at me.

"Is your dad ready?" I ask.

She points at a pair of cylindrical vacuum cleaners, the ones you see at car washes. I look over and see Mr. Lee meticulously cleaning the cylinders.

"He may take a while again," Amanda says. "He told us to wait inside until he's done."

When I enter through the screen door into the kitchen, I see Mrs. Lee is cutting chicken again. She sees me and pauses, raising her head in acknowledgement.

"I loved the chicken feet. It was the best dinner I had in awhile," I say to her.

"Oh, that's great! Thank you! I'm glad you liked it," she says, smiling and nodding her head. "Do you want some water?"

Amanda and I settle on the restaurant's booths gripping our styrofoam cups. Shortly after, Mrs. Lee comes from the kitchen and hands us a bowl of grapes.

Thirty minutes later, Mr. Lee enters the dining area and settles down in the same metal chair from the previous interview. Again, Amanda stands up to disappear into the kitchen.

"Any updates on your project? What do you think so far?" he asks.

"The Honors College accepted my proposal, and I've transcribed last time's audio, but that's about it," I say.

The conversation shifts towards me as he starts asking me about the Philippines, my country of birth. He mentions that he used to live there as a refugee, but that would be a story for a later time. Then he describes how he entered the restaurant business in Arkansas by working under his Uncle Qiang, his sponsor that enabled him to immigrate to the United States. Mr. Lee eventually left the restaurant business to pursue a career as a mechanic before serving in the U.S. Navy. When neither of those panned out, he returned to the restaurant business with a friend, another refugee from the Khmer Rouge, and opened Fu Lin in Conway. It was there that he met and married Mrs. Lee. In time, he and his family rented out what used to be a post office so he could convert it into what it is today: Oriental Kitchen.

As we continue to ramble, the atmosphere feels less tense, and I begin to feel less apprehensive. I assumed our interactions required a level of formality since this is a thesis project, but Mr. Lee lets me bring my guard down. He's humorous, grounded, and an enthusiastic conversationalist. It is apparent while talking to him that he is a successful small business owner, and if it wasn't for Amanda, I would've never guessed that he was a refugee.

"Any Cambodian that is in my generation… well, I don't know about other Asians, but when Cambodians were making money, they bought gold. They don't put it in the bank," Mr. Lee says.

"Even when they came to America?" I ask.

"Yes, we go to the jewelry store because to them it feels more secure. We grew up in wars, and every time war starts, currency becomes useless. Only gold, jewelry, and watches were useful."

Back at the village, the wealthy from Phnom Penh had plenty of gold and jewelry, which they exchanged with the rural villagers for bamboo and leaves to build shelters. One group of wealthier people pushed their car under the impression that everyone was returning to Phnom Penh. They stored all of their belongings in it, so they too had a lot of gold and jewelry to exchange for materials and laborers. Even in a so-called communist utopia, the wealthier still had an advantage as everyone was expected to build their own shelters without being provided the necessary materials.

During the trek down Highway One, Guang found and recognized the owners of Dak's former company. Despite having to close down, they were still a wealthy family, and it showed because the French car they pushed was built like a Rolls Royce with the status of a Mercedes Benz. Dak's former bosses loved Guang; nobody in the neighborhood possessed an ill thought about her. As a result, they offered that the Lees accompany them when it came time to build a shelter because they had access to gold and other valuables. Dak's bosses traded some of their gold to hire laborers, and asked them to build the Lee's shelter right next to theirs. The shelter had no walls, and consisted of six bamboo posts supporting a roof made from large leaves and straw. It was enough for the seven of them to fit. Once again, the only thing covering the family was the mosquito net and that worn out blanket, but at least the rain didn't hit them directly anymore.

The next day, the leader of the village approached the citizens of Phnom Penh, and he told them if they worked, they would receive food to eat. The crowd perked up because food was so scarce. Every able-bodied person offered their help, including Mr. Lee and his family.

Mr. Lee's job was to cut wild grass about six feet tall with a scythe provided to him by the villagers. He worked from sunrise to sunset. Due to exhaustion and famine, many around him passed out. At the end of the day, Mr. Lee lined up for the much-anticipated food: a small, 3-ounce cup containing a mix of corn, wheat, and rice inside. To Mr. Lee's dismay, it was nowhere near fresh. The pieces of corn were hollow inside because worms had eaten through it. The rice was either raw, or half cooked. Mr. Lee was so hungry though; he had no choice but to eat it. He returned to Guang and the rest of his family and showed them his cup where he realized they all had the same rations.

The family decided to soak their food in water which they placed in a small pot Guang had traded for with some of the little gold she had. Soaking the food killed the worms by waiting for them to drown and float up to the surface. Then the Lees used the same pot to boil the rations. This became a daily routine as the food never improved. Mr. Lee remembered having severe diarrhea, but at least those meager rations gave him enough energy to survive.

In the fields, it was rare for Mr. Lee to encounter wild grass shorter than him. Most of the time he was cutting it blind since he couldn't see over the top. There were some days where Mr. Lee would hear explosions, but he didn't know where they came from or what they were. At times he would be 10 feet away from an explosion, close enough to hear the sharp whizzing sound of shrapnel. Seconds later, he would see a cloud of black smoke rise to the sky. Finally, one day the local villagers unearthed a warhead in the grassy field, and they displayed it at the entrance to the field. Mr. Lee eventually learned that these unexploded warheads were dropped during the Civil War and continued to detonate, thus explaining the explosions.

"I wish we had cell phones to take pictures of it," Mr. Lee says as he starts laughing. He pretends to take a picture with an imaginary phone in his hand. I start laughing despite the morbidity of it all.

The true injustice came from the village leaders. For in this new society which preached a communist ideology of equality, the higher-ups in the village were large and muscular, a sign they were being fed a sufficient amount of food in addition to also living in nice wooden houses. Not only were they better fed and sheltered, but they often looted people's dwellings, robbing them of what little they had left. Meanwhile, the Phnom Penh arrivals looked like skeletons with flesh clinging to their bones. They were dying every day. Some committed suicide either by hanging themselves or ingesting poisonous plants in the wild. Others died from malaria, starvation or execution as gunshots added to the daily drone of everyday life in the village. A family living across from the Lees started out as 13 members. Eventually, it shrank to just one teenage boy about Seng's age. One day, Mr. Lee walked up to him and asked why he was alone.

"They're all dead. There was one day where three of them died," he said.

The crying also became more rampant as more and more people were losing family members. The once-a-day rations were now only three ounces of rice, and if they were lucky, it was garnished with a wild vegetable. It was never enough to satisfy Mr. Lee's hunger, and at times he could even count how many grains of rice he had. The very least they could've done, Mr. Lee thought, was to cook it properly, but often the rice was mostly cloudy water. Guang worried for her children, so she sometimes gave them her portions, before falling asleep crying. Mr. Lee had to accept it but could not bear to watch his mother sacrifice what little she already had. His hands would shake when he ate.

He started to look like a skeleton along with the rest of the newcomers. To survive, Mr. Lee caught frogs in the night-time. He would chop their heads off, peel off their skin and then cook it all in the fire.

"It was like *Naked and Afraid*. Have you ever seen the show?" I shake my head no. "Really? You've never seen the show?" Mr. Lee asks.

"So, were you naked when you were eating these frogs?"

Mr. Lee starts laughing again. "No, it's just like the show though. You eat anything on site… if it looks edible."

Eventually though, the harsh conditions wore on Mr. Lee, drowning him in despair. He woke up with the sole purpose of survival and went to bed hungry, only to wake up hours later to repeat the same torment. For Mr. Lee, it would have been more bearable to know when it would end; however, no end was in sight.

"Over 40 years later, whenever I restock my container in the kitchen with rice, I sometimes still cry. I still think about that suffering there," Mr. Lee says. He does not laugh.

As time passed, Guang's mosquito net started showing signs of wear-and-tear. The net started ripping, making holes large enough for the mosquitos to penetrate. Guang used the cloth from old clothes to patch these holes up. It helped, but Mr. Lee still had to be careful not to lean his body too close to the net. Otherwise he would feel thousands of mosquitos, their fangs like needles piercing him.

Sometimes when Mr. Lee would relieve himself in the wilderness, the mosquitos would attack him, causing even the most hidden parts of his body to itch uncontrollably. The mosquitos seemed to be as hungry for blood as the people were for food.

"I still have the scars on my butt from when I went to the bathroom. They were like vampires." Mr. Lee says.

One day, a village leader called for a group meeting. Next to him was a civilian from Phnom Penh, his skeleton body lying on the dirt with his hands and feet tied.

"Last night, this man stole a chicken," the leader said.

Mr. Lee understood. He knew the man was starving. Everyone was.

"By the order of *Angka*, we will now punish him."

The other soldiers stripped the man naked and tied him onto a wooden pole. The village leader said he would stay on the pole for 24 hours. If the thief could survive the night, then he would be allowed to live. Mr. Lee was confused at the sheer nature of such a punishment. What could possibly happen overnight to suggest that the man might not survive?

The next morning Mr. Lee's question was answered when he went to the wooden pole to check on the chicken thief. The man's body was a pale white, and all over he was covered in mosquito bites. It seemed like thousands of those vampire mosquitos drained him of all his blood. He looked like he had been dead for a while. Mr. Lee never knew the name of the village he was stationed to work at, but after all of his experience with these winged devils, he decided to call it Mosquito Village.

As time passed, the death toll continued to rise. There were days where Mr. Lee and other younger children were assigned to carry the dead away on metal sheets, usually two children holding the sheet for one dead body. One child hoisted from the front, the other from the back. On one particular day, Mr. Lee and his partner were carrying away an older woman when he stumbled from chronic fatigue and malnutrition. As a result, the woman rolled off the sheet. When he and his partner hoisted her back onto the sheet, Mr. Lee felt how cold and stiff her body had become.

"I said sorry to her and we kept moving. May God have mercy on her," Mr. Lee says.

On August 19th, 1975, a few months after the takeover of Phnom Penh, Prince Sihanouk was convinced to return and be head of state despite his disapproval of the regime. He served as a puppet to legitimize the Khmer Rouge to the population and even represented Cambodia at the United Nations. Meanwhile, as an effort to better control the entire population and open new areas for agricultural production, the Khmer Rouge initiated a second major transfer of population towards the end of the year, the first having occurred with the displacement of citizens from Phnom Penh and other cities to the southern part of the country. However, these areas soon became overcrowded. This second transfer was to scatter the population into more spacious parts to the north and east of the country.

For Mr. Lee and his family, the end of 1975 marked several months at Mosquito Village. One day, Mr. Lee returned from work with his brothers and sisters to find out many Phnom Penh residents were preparing to leave. Mr. Lee started asking around, trying to find out where they were going. Nobody knew, except that everybody would be leaving first thing the next morning.

As soon as the sun rose, the survivors of Mosquito Village trekked 10 kilometers to a bank on the Mekong river where three boats large enough to seat at least 100 people were docked and waiting for them. Throughout the journey, Mr. Lee watched as the group of survivors dwindled, as many were led to another riverbank. The sun had set, but instead of the moon, storm clouds swarmed the sky. It started to rain, and Mr. Lee had nothing to cover himself with. When it finally stopped, Mr. Lee was left shivering.

Mr. Lee arrived at a riverbank, and it took hours until the Khmer Rouge soldiers there began forcing people into the first of three boats. A few hours after sunset, Mr. Lee noticed an old lady crying. She was balling up scraps of paper and throwing them into a fire. Curious, Mr. Lee walked closer to her to investigate. The lady had a big bag where she reached down to pull out some brightly colored paper. Upon closer inspection, those scraps of paper she was balling up were

100 to 500 *riels* in bills, currency that had long been useless. Money had become so worthless that it was more beneficial to use as tinder. There was a little pot of boiling water over the fire she was maintaining.

Eventually, everyone had to form a line and wait until they could board the boat. Some people who were boarding the first boat had suitcases, bags, and buckets full of *riels*. When the Khmer Rouge soldiers searched their belongings inside the boat, they started yelling at them, throwing the luggage—including the buckets of money—off the boat. Mr. Lee watched as cash went flying before floating down the river.

Remembering Dak's words, the priority was to keep the family together. Dak's bosses had separated from the Lees, but they were still intact which was all that mattered. When Mr. Lee reached the front of the line, the first boat had already left. The second boat was almost at full capacity, and the Khmer Rouge soldiers were yelling that there were only three seats left.

"Should three of us board, and the rest go on the next boat?" Seng asked.

"No," Mr. Lee said sternly. "We're all boarding together." There was no guarantee the boats would all have the same destination. It was better to not take any chances.

Finally, the Lee family boarded the third and final boat. As soon as everyone was seated and settled, an exhausted Mr. Lee fell asleep.

It was daylight when he woke up. The other two boats that had left in front of them were nowhere to be seen. A few hours passed when commotion suddenly grew amongst the passengers. Visible off the coast was the skyline of Phnom Penh. The people on board could not contain their excitement, thinking that the nightmare was at last over. Some cheered and others started grabbing their belongings, ready to escape back to their old homes as soon as the boat docked. The Khmer Rouge, however, had other ideas. As the boat eased closer to the coast, it turned away from the city. Everyone on board grew silent as despair filled the air once again. Mr. Lee started to hear the all too familiar sound of crying. As the tall buildings of Phnom Penh shrank, the crying was broken by screams of passengers jumping overboard into the strong currents of the river.

The boat continued north for another full day. In between that time, Khmer Rouge soldiers came by and handed each passenger a loaf of bread. Mr. Lee, believing they weren't planning on feeding him again, nibbled at it to keep his stomach from feeling completely empty. He was right; it was the only source of food for 48 hours. At the end of the two-day journey, all of the passengers disembarked onto a small village where everyone would temporarily stay at a destroyed Buddhist temple.

The temple was abandoned and had fallen into disrepair; had holes where sunlight and rain could penetrate. The routine remained the same as in Mosquito Village. The soldiers told everyone they would receive food rations if they worked the whole day, and for Mr. Lee, the job was mainly to chop tall grass. Guang still had the small pot from Mosquito Village to cook food, boil water, and use as a basin to wash clothes. There was also an abundance of firewood in the nearby jungle.

Mr. Lee met a teenage girl around the same age as him named Leng who was also Chinese-Cambodian. The only family she had left was her little 5-year-old brother, Dang, and her mother. The rest had either died or had been separated. One day, Leng approached Mr. Lee while he was working and asked him if he had seen her mother.

"She said she was headed to the river to fetch us water, but when I returned at night, she was still gone," she said. Leng searched the riverbank the night before to no avail as her absence grew. Mr. Lee decided to try his luck and went to the riverbank. He asked the laborers working there if they had seen an older, fair-skinned woman the day before. One of the men spoke up.

"I saw a woman jump into the river from a nearby cliff," he said. "It may have been her."

At night after work, Mr. Lee found Leng with her brother in the temple and relayed what information he had. Leng curled into a ball and cried into her arms as Dang watched her. Mr. Lee couldn't hold back his tears either. He remembered Gia. He understood the pain of uncertainty not knowing if a loved-one was dead or alive. As he cried, he was also reminded that he was starving. Starving for over half a year now. He remembered his father in Vietnam, and Heng in Macau, both not with him and the rest of his family. Life had drastically changed, and everything seemed hopeless.

"It was so sad, man. Man, everything was so sad," Mr. Lee says.

Time passed when one morning a wave of army trucks appeared at the abandoned temple. Trucks meant bad news, and Mr. Lee started to tremble. The rumor was that once someone was loaded into a truck, it meant execution.

"Time to move!" The Khmer Rouge soldiers announced from their megaphones.

With no choice but to follow orders, Mr. Lee gathered his family and made sure everyone boarded the same truck. Leng and Dang boarded the truck behind them. The engines roared, and Mr. Lee watched as the ruins of the abandoned temple shrank until they were completely behind him, replaced by the dirt road, wilderness, and the anxiety of what was to come next.

BRAVE VILLAGE

I T'S MONDAY AFTERNOON in the middle of October when I enter Oriental Kitchen not through the back screen-door, but through the entrance. Today I am not an interviewer, but a customer. Inside is a small crowd of people sitting in the same booths and chairs Amanda and Mr. Lee had been sitting in. Others were standing in the corner waiting for their take-out orders. It's a strange feeling being here during opening hours because I'm used to this room being empty. I ring the bell on the open rectangular frame carved in the front wall, and Mrs. Lee appears.

"Oh Kenny. How are you? Are you here to order something?"

"General Tso's please."

"Ok, it will be about 30 minutes."

I pay my less than $10 tab and take a seat at the same place I conduct my interviews with Mr. Lee which had recently been vacated by a customer. I observe as some people claim their orders and then talk to Mrs. Lee with a sense of familiarity. Every time an order is ready, she peeks her head from behind the wall frame to bring out a plastic bag with to-go boxes inside. She calls out people's names as they come to the front. Since it is peak dinner hours, the place is constantly filled with customers. For such a small space hidden from the main road by a gas station, Oriental Kitchen does not struggle with attracting customers. Finally, Mrs. Lee calls my name, and I walk up to the front.

"I gave you a free egg roll. Thanks for coming." Mrs. Lee is always trying to make me feel guilty. Even when I order like a regular customer, I leave with some free food.

"Yeah we like to give big portions," Mr. Lee says, as he laughs in his chair. I am explaining the events of this past Monday to him. When I returned home to start eating, I never realized how big my order was. I thought the styrofoam to-go box would include my rice and the General Tso's. However, the entire box was filled to the brim with General Tso's. If I pushed my fork into the bed of chicken, the sauce would spill out onto the table. When I looked in the plastic bag again, I grabbed a cardboard oyster pail which was also filled to the brim with steaming hot white rice. On top of that was Mrs.

Lee's complimentary egg roll, and I thought to myself, how was I supposed to finish this?

The answer was I didn't.

"I had to share it with a friend," I say. It may be a reach to say their portions stem from the hunger they faced when they were younger, but they may be a symbol of never going back to those days of starvation felt under the Khmer Rouge. Or maybe meat is just cheap and I'm reading too much into it, but my interviews with Mr. Lee can't help but prompt some questioning on my end.

"Siem Reap is where you visited right?" Mr. Lee asks me.

I nod.

"The trucks took us to the province of Preah Vihear, the densest jungle in all of Cambodia, and it is next to Siem Reap," he says. Preah Vihear is located in the north-central zone of Cambodia, bordering Thailand. Under the Khmer Rouge, the province was region or *Damban* 103.

The journey to Preah Vihear was a long one since they had to travel up north from an area closer to Phnom Penh. The trucks took Mr. Lee's group through unpaved dirt roads and jungles previously untouched by humankind. The soldiers provided food, but sparingly. They only gave raw rice so

Guang had to cook it herself. Other than to eat, the soldiers stopped the truck only for bathroom breaks.

"We were like dogs. We weren't human beings anymore," Mr. Lee says, as he chuckles.

The trucks stopped at a village one night where everyone was to stay until the next morning. There was a pond inviting the travelers to take a bath, and it also provided them with edible lotus roots. As Mr. Lee soaked his body, he suddenly heard screams pierce the air.

"Someone is drowning!"

Mr. Lee rushed over to the commotion and found a crowd of people staring off into the deep end of the pond. There were people in the area who saw the poor soul drown, but nobody had the energy to dive in for a rescue. Maybe they thought the person was better off dead than staying alive in this hell. Mr. Lee was told by witnesses that it was a girl, no older than 14 years old. He was bathing with all of his siblings, so he knew it wasn't Guah. Then he noticed Dang by himself.

"It can't be," Mr. Lee said. He searched the crowd of people for Leng, only to find out she had gone missing from the group. At 5 years old, Dang was all alone. He had lost his mother and now his sister.

When the army trucks left the village, they started dispersing onto different roads meaning they were all headed towards separate villages. Dang's truck had also split from Mr. Lee's, which meant he never saw Dang again. Mr. Lee, along with a few other trucks, arrived at another destroyed temple. The soldiers told everyone they had to eat immediately because they wouldn't be staying at the temple for long.

The soldiers were right. In 10 minutes as everyone finished gathering firewood, the Khmer Rouge soldiers returned with oxcarts and ordered that everyone had to leave. After travelling for about 30 minutes by oxen, the Lee family arrived at another makeshift shack, similar to the one at Mosquito Village except this shack was longer and had walls. The seven of them had to share the shack with four other families. It was almost dark outside as everyone started settling in with their belongings. Suddenly, three muscular men with no shirts and rifles strapped diagonally on their chest came inside the shack.

"This is an order from *Angka*. Whoever is against *Angka* will find death." The muscular soldiers started searching everyone's belongings looking for any contraband they considered dangerous. The soldiers explained that everything in the community was shared. Mr. Lee describes the Khmer

Rouge's vision for equality as "one family, one heart, one mind, one body."

The three men led the new arrivals to a town hall which also functioned as a communal cafeteria. It was a small open shack with a few long benches and tables. Here, everyone had to eat together. It was time for dinner, and to Mr. Lee's surprise, it actually felt like one.

"It wasn't a great meal, but to us this was some damn good food. It was the best meal we had had for a year. I got enough rice to stuff my stomach. We had chicken, banana, flour, and squash. I still wasn't full though, maybe about 70%," Mr. Lee says.

Mr. Lee was assigned to a village collective divided into three smaller villages: Brave, Perseverance, and Victory. Prior to Mr. Lee's arrival, each of these villages consisted of about 100 inhabitants. The shack that was the Lee's new home was part of Brave Village. After all the newcomers from Phnom Penh moved in, he estimated that the population jumped to around 600 inhabitants.

Mr. Lee's shack was situated right outside the village center where most of the bamboo and wood houses were located. These were inhabited by the rural people who already resided in the area prior to the Khmer Rouge's rise to power. All the newcomers from Phnom Penh were segregated outside of the center into a shantytown.

The next morning, Mr. Lee was awakened to the sound of a metal instrument hitting a car rim as the sun rose over the horizon. One of the soldiers entered the shack Mr. Lee was staying in and ordered them to the town hall.

There Mr. Lee joined a hodgepodge of newcomers and original inhabitants of the village. Many of the indigenous people in the village were all dark-skinned with curly hair, and most did not wear shirts. A few black-uniformed village leaders standing in front of town hall were awaiting everyone's arrival. They were Brave Village's superiors.

"For all the new people, when the bell rings it's time to work," one of them said.

As each leader took turns introducing themselves, Mr. Lee noticed they kept referring to the people from the cities as "new people" and the indigenous villagers as "old people."

When the speeches concluded, soldiers on the ground began splitting the new arrivals into two groups based on physical size: children and adults. People deemed as children were allowed to eat breakfast and asked to report to school where their teachers would watch over them. The adults received no breakfast and were divided into different jobs.

Mr. Lee was assigned to harvest rice. When he arrived on the field after the meeting for his first day of work, the Khmer Rouge soldier in charge gave everyone sickles to reap the rice crop. Being from the city, handling the sharp blade of a sickle proved too problematic for Mr. Lee. He cut his finger, instantly drawing blood, and since there were no bandages around, he pulled out a piece of grass from the ground and chewed on it, using the bolus to plug his wound.

At the end of the day, Mr. Lee talked about his experience with the rest of his family. Guang shared that she had to cross the river on a big log, and nobody had bothered to flatten it, making it easy for the newcomers to slip and fall. Since Guang belonged to the "new people," she didn't have the experience to navigate this rural society. "I watched as some people walked on it with ease, while someone had to hold my hand," she said.

Once again, Mr. Lee fell into a routine revolving around intense physical labor although it was a bit better compared to Mosquito Village. Since he was considered an adult, he skipped breakfast and immediately went to work in the fields, but at least this time he was able to eat two meals a day: lunch and dinner.

The meals were usually rice porridge sometimes accompanied with wild vegetables. If Mr. Lee was lucky, the village would kill a chicken for everyone to eat. Despite the Khmer Rouge's vision of equality, the women serving food from in the kitchen discriminated against the "new people." There were times when Mr. Lee and other newcomers would purposefully get scooped little to no food while their darker-skinned counterparts were given larger portions.

The soldiers also required all "new people" to wear the Khmer Rouge uniform of black clothes and a long red and white checkered scarf called a *krama*. Since there were no black shirts, they were given a white one and shown how to dye it black. Everyone had to soak it in the mud until it turned brown dark enough to be considered black.

"I don't know why they like black, man. Those soldiers, *Angka*, whatever. If you wore black, you apparently felt really proud of yourself. They gave me one white shirt and a pair of shorts for the whole year. No underwear. No shoes," Mr. Lee says.

Mr. Lee was working on the field when he heard the call for lunch. He arrived at the town hall and walked past some food laying out on a flat board of bamboo. As Mr. Lee ate lunch, a Khmer Rouge soldier approached him and pulled him aside.

"Someone reported that you kicked dirt into the food," he said.

Panic mingled with confusion rose up in Mr. Lee. The force from the soldier's grab caused him to drop his plate of food. Mr. Lee would later learn that the "old people" liked to set their food low to the ground, so he had to walk past it slowly or else he may inadvertently kick dirt into it. At the time Mr. Lee was clueless.

"You know, because you did that, I could punch you once and finish you alive. Then, I would hang you upside-down and feed you to the ants. However, I will let you go this time," the soldier said.

He was a giant man, and he probably meant it when he said he could finish Mr. Lee off in one punch. He had become less of a skeleton, but his body was still weak. Mr. Lee could still remember how heavy his chest felt.

"Every day, I had to learn how to be smarter in order to stay alive..." he says.

Guang tried her best to keep up with her new role as a community cook. She was entrusted to prepare meals and fetch ingredients and firewood from the jungle because the people in the village provided very little to cook with. There were harvests, but somehow food was still scarce. Although Guang worked hard, coming from Phnom Penh meant she was not used to this kind of labor. Everyone working with her knew.

Guang's co-workers had been mainly "old people" from the village. Two of them had been working pregnant, and they recently gave birth to their newborns. Since everyone in the household had to work in the name of *Angka*, nobody was able to look after them. As a result, both ended up bringing their babies to work where they were confined to a towel placed on the floor, left almost entirely unsupervised. Their anguished wails pierced the air without relenting, adding to the existing background chorus of chaos.

The new mothers needed to do something with their newborns. They looked over at Guang who was still struggling in the kitchen and came to her with a proposition: babysit the kids.

Guang did not hesitate to agree. After all, she loved babies, and from her experience in Phnom Penh, babies loved her back. Being a caretaker was a role she was confident in. Over the next few days, Guang watched over both of her co-workers' babies in the corner of the kitchen while they both worked. Guang bathed and cleaned them and crisscrossed her legs to let them sleep there instead of on the hard floor. Miraculously, the babies stopped crying. The mothers noticed this. The other cooks noticed it. Even their kitchen leader noticed it who later informed the other village higher-ups, enabling Guang to officially change her position.

Guang started living full time in the shack to fulfill her babysitting duties. She first received babies from villagers before they headed to work and cared for them until the parents returned later at night. At first, Guang only had the two babies from her former co-workers at the kitchens, but over time she slowly accepted or was assigned more.

At the shack, she used the red-checkered *kramas* to make hammocks for the babies to sleep in. She weaved vines or the strings from the rice bags into a rope and used it to tie the *krama* from end-to-end on the bamboo poles supporting the shack. The makeshift hammocks helped the babies sleep soundly. Guang saw how malnourished they were, so she tried her best to at least give them a good rest. She never allowed a baby to sleep on the dirt floor.

Over time, Guang's reputation grew, and people started bringing their children to her. All of a sudden, Guang was taking care of over 10 babies, and the shack was so tangled with hammock lines, Mr. Lee and his siblings could barely move around.

"Mother, you're taking care of too many babies," Mr. Lee said.

"It's OK son. Just be careful and duck underneath or step over the ropes," Guang replied.

One of the village leaders heard of Guang's work as she slowly became famous throughout the village. One day, he decided to visit her, bringing his small baby girl. Even though Guang was overrun with babies, she could and would not refuse one. She became known as Grandma Guang.

Grandma Guang's popularity set the precedent for other women to be assigned as babysitters. Some of the "new people" in the shantytown started to resent Guang, even showing her public displays of animosity. The idea that Guang, who was taken captive by the Khmer Rouge, was openly trying her best to take care of their babies did not sit well with the newcomers. She had some newborns from "new people," but most of her babies were from the village. It didn't help her image when she even accepted one from a village leader, although Mr. Lee doubted she had a choice. To the "new people" it felt like betrayal, but Guang didn't care. She worked to the best of her ability for the babies' welfare.

There was a Chinese woman in the shantytown who was also assigned to be a babysitter. She was known to have an nasty personality, and one time she confronted Guang.

"Evil people ordered you to do this job," she said. "Why do you care so much about babies that aren't yours?"

Guang immediately retaliated.

"What the hell are you talking about? Babies are innocent. A baby is just a baby, and it doesn't matter whose it is. Just because some of these babies were born from killers doesn't mean they're evil like their parents. Babies are born innocent."

Mr. Lee believed the Chinese woman was jealous because she was known to be pretty mean to the children she took care of. Rumors were also spreading that babies taken care of by other sitters were abused. Nobody could give them the attention they needed because all their energy went to taking care of their stomachs.

The other four families living with the Lees didn't seem to mind the overflow of babies onto their side of the shack. Usually everyone was out working, so they hardly had to see them anyway. Among one of the families living with Mr. Lee was a former soldier of Lon Nol, a Khmer man named Dara.

Dara was naturally a bully, always trying to pick a fight, and he enjoyed ordering people around, including Mr. Lee. There was one instance when Mr. Lee was resting in the shack after a long day at the fields when Dara barked at him to go fetch a stick. Mr. Lee didn't want to pick a fight, so he grudgingly went outside to look for one. When he found a suitable one, he gave it to Dara who started scratching himself with it. Mr. Lee was so annoyed at how lazy the man was. He figured Dara was probably a high ranking official under Lon Nol, and was therefore used to bossing people around.

One night there was a bad storm, torrents of rain beating down upon the village. It was late, and Guang had not eaten dinner yet because there were babies yet to be picked up by their mothers. One of the villagers stopped by and told Guang that the town hall was saving her dinner. When the last child was finally claimed, Guang readied herself to brace the storm. Mr. Lee was in his corner of the shack, watching her.

"Mother are you going to be comfortable going by yourself?" he asked.

"Yes, son, I will be fine."

As more time passed and Guang had not returned, Mr. Lee and his siblings started to worry. When they decided to search for her outside, a dark figure emerged at the shack's entrance. It was a man, and he was carrying someone in his arms. The man was Dara, and he was carrying an unconscious Guang. Her body was wet from the rain, and she was covered in mud. Mr. Lee began to shake because his mother could be dying. Dara explained that on his way back from town hall, he saw Guang unconscious and face down on the dirt road. He thought she had tripped and hit her head on something because it was so dark and stormy.

"If I had not been there, she would've suffocated. She had mud covering her nose and mouth," Dara said.

News had spread fast in the village, and not long after Dara came, village leaders, along with muscular Khmer Rouge soldiers, swarmed the shack. Mr. Lee recognized the one leader that usually left his little daughter with Guang, and Mr. Lee watched as the man ordered everyone but Guang's children out of the shack. The leader pulled out a small container from his pant pocket.

"I couldn't believe this man. The leader took out some pills. Western medicine! I could tell he really loved my mom," Mr. Lee says.

Guang was still unconscious so it was impossible for her to take the medicine. Dara, who was still in the room, instinctively grabbed one of Guang's hands and pressed hard on her thumb. All the village leaders were startled as Guang started stirring. Dara helped her sit up and as she looked around at all the village leaders, she started spewing incoherent insults at everyone, words that probably would have gotten any other person executed. Instead, everyone started laughing. Guang eventually recognized the leader as the one who usually brought his daughter for babysitting.

"Please you need to eat something," he said to her. "You can rest tonight and tomorrow."

As the situation started to calm down, all the village leaders started focusing their attention on Dara. The former soldier stared back at them. One of the leaders finally spoke up.

"Hey sir, we need to talk to you."

"Can I have my dinner first?" Dara asked. His dinner plate was tucked in-between his shorts and his abdomen.

"No, it won't take long," the soldier said.

The soldier lied. Dara never returned to the shack that night. He didn't return the day after either. Mr. Lee eventually heard rumors that some of the villagers were out hunting when they saw Dara's chopped head hanging from a tree. All because they found out he used to fight for the enemy.

SCHOOL

ON JANUARY 5TH 1976, the Khmer Rouge officially named their controlled land the Democratic Kampuchea. Two months later, Prince Sihanouk was asked to resign and was later placed under house arrest. Pol Pot would assume power as prime minister. Meanwhile, Mr. Lee continued his day-to-day life in Brave Village where he noticed how isolated the "old people" were from urban life. One day, he was chopping trees in the jungle when an army truck approached the village. He watched as the village children dropped grass by the tires of the parked truck. Mr. Lee went over and asked them what they were doing. One kid said he was feeding the animal.

"Look at it. It's so big!" the boy said.

They thought the truck was an animal. Mr. Lee realized they had never seen a car before. Shaking his head in bewilderment, Mr. Lee returned to his task of chopping trees. The goal was to clear land for more farming space. Like the sickle, Mr. Lee had no experience wielding an axe. As he tried to chop a log in half, he instead swung down onto his foot.

Mr. Lee stops the story and shows me the scar on his right foot.

"The cut was so deep that I saw one of my veins," he says.

Blood was gushing everywhere. Mr. Lee dropped to the ground howling in pain. Two of the nearby village nurses rushed to the scene. When they examined his leg, they ran away screaming at the sight of blood. Mr. Lee raised his voice again, this time a hint of frustration mingled with his agony. He sounded like a disgruntled customer complaining to the staff at the front desk. "I'm like, what the hell man! How are you a nurse if you're scared of blood?" Mr. Lee is practically shouting in his chair at this point.

Mr. Lee clutched his leg, writhing in pain for what seemed like hours until help eventually arrived in the form of a man, one of the "older people." Without uttering a word, the man grabbed Mr. Lee, placed him on his back, and carried him to the local hospital.

At the hospital, they were approached by an older nurse. She led the two to an open space where Mr. Lee could lie down. The floor was made of wood, and there was a long sheet used as Mr. Lee's bed. Although uncomfortable, it was still better than sleeping on dirt. The nurse's aged appearance indicated she was more experienced as she did not run away from the blood. Instead, she stopped the bleeding by placing animal ash on Mr. Lee's wound. The man smiled at Mr. Lee and left.

"I will never forget that man. I hope one day that I can go see him," Mr. Lee says, his tone becoming more serious.

For the first week, Mr. Lee was in agonizing pain. The hospital didn't have painkillers or antibiotics to treat the wound. All they did was stop the bleeding with ash. Mr. Lee couldn't walk; he could barely use the restroom. However, the stay wasn't all bad. The hospital fed him greater portions compared to what he would normally get at the dining hall. He also didn't have to work.

Mr. Lee would inform the soldier watching him if he was sick, allowing him to rest for the day. However, if he kept making excuses without any solid evidence, he would be taken into the jungle to be executed.

"Leave you around, nothing gained. Take you away, nothing lost. That was their quote," Mr. Lee says.

It was during the second week that Mr. Lee started to recover, and by the end of the 14 days, he was discharged. He was able to walk, but he still hobbled. He was careful not to put too much pressure on his right foot because it was still healing, and he was scared that if he placed it under too much force, the wound would open up again. There was a little bit of pus on it, but otherwise the foot would manage. Mr. Lee knew he had to be tough. Living in Democratic Kampuchea meant he had to be responsible for his own life.

The sound of metal hitting a car rim pierced the air at dawn. For the first time in two weeks, Mr. Lee would report to work in the field again. Guang was upset he didn't stay in the hospital longer, but Mr. Lee didn't want to appear lazy in front of the village. When Mr. Lee told one of the soldiers he was ready to work, the soldier looked at his condition and told him he should be assigned to go to school with the younger kids instead. Mr. Lee was apparently in no condition to work all day in the field.

The so-called school in Brave Village was an old two-story Buddhist temple that had been partially destroyed and ransacked. The first floor was for instruction and the second floor for sleeping. Mr. Lee compared the experience to being shipped off to boarding school.

Since Mr. Lee was now considered a child due to his status as a student, he was able to eat breakfast every morning around sunrise. Afterwards, they started classes on the first floor and were segregated into classrooms for boys and girls.

There were five class sections in total, three sections of boys taught by male teachers, and two sections of girls taught by female teachers who all looked like they were in their twenties and were all from the village.

At this point, Mr. Lee was approximately 16 years old. Even though he was small in stature, only a few kids matched his size. There were children in his class as young as five years old. Mr. Lee's teacher was a man named Prak, and every day he would teach the students Khmer and very basic math. The students had pens and paper only available when Prak provided for them since supplies were so limited. The education was poor by Mr. Lee's standards. All the students who lived in Phnom Penh knew more than Prak, sometimes even helping him solve his own questions. The math problems were as elementary as they came:

"There are 6 people in the house, and each person should get 2 bowls of rice. How many bowls of rice does each person get?"

All the "old people" students including Prak counted on their fingers. Mr. Lee laughed in his head because using that method meant they were going to run out of fingers.

At around noon, the students were served lunch, and an hour after eating, everyone had to work in the fields until nightfall, sometimes going late into the night. After field work was finished, there was dinner and then a meeting where all the teachers would discuss the good and the bad events of the day. The teachers would ask the students to criticize each other, but hardly anyone spoke up, so the meetings were very short.

After lunch one afternoon, all the teachers in the school held a special meeting before starting field work. While Mr. Lee and the rest of the students were outside, the instructors were presented with large bottles of a light pink fluid. Prak and all the other teachers had everyone line up and drink about an ounce of it using hollow bamboo cups. The smell was repulsive, and when Mr. Lee received his serving, he could barely look at it. As he chugged it, he held his breath and closed his eyes.

"Whoo, that was probably one of the bitterest things I ever drank. The other kids around me spat it out, while others couldn't help but vomit. I tried not to vomit because it was against *Angka*," Mr. Lee says.

Prak then explained that the fluid came from a human gallbladder, and that's when Mr. Lee noticed a greenish tinge from a small stone inside the bottles.

Mr. Lee laughs.

"Sometimes I wished I disobeyed *Angka*, especially after he told me."

Mr. Lee had never been placed in a position where he had to learn Khmer, especially since he lived in a tight-knit Chinese neighborhood within Phnom Penh. After living in rural Democratic Kampuchea for almost two years, he became fluent in the language. He made friends who had a Khmer heritage, and all his superiors were Khmer. The Khmer classes at school also helped. He avoided speaking Mandarin or Teochew because the soldiers may become suspicious of him. Thankfully, Mr. Lee did not know Vietnamese and the soldiers never found out he had family in Vietnam, as the country was perceived as a pressing threat to the Khmer Rouge's sovereignty.

Mr. Lee met a Khmer boy also from Phnom Penh in his class who was a little younger and smaller in size than him. His name was Samang and like all the other schoolchildren from the city, they both faced discrimination and mistreatment. Sometimes teachers forced them to work extra hours in the field while allowing indigenous children to finish the day and eat first.

On the field, nobody was separated by gender, nationality, or physical ability. All children worked together in the afternoon. Mr. Lee would always try to work close to Samang and the other city-dwelling children because the villagers never welcomed them. Mr. Lee remembers a girl named Soriya who was about 13 years old. She was the daughter of one of the village leaders which gave her a little bit of a superiority complex. Upon seeing them, her face would scowl before calling Mr. Lee and the "new people" ugly or stupid. One day, all the children had to chop weeds from the soil with hoes. Mr. Lee had no prior experience, so naturally he struggled at first. He was working next to Soriya, and as usual she presented a very ugly demeanor, as if she didn't want to be seen working next to someone who was beneath her. Mr. Lee ignored her because he was too preoccupied learning how to swing the hoe.

When Mr. Lee felt like he had mastered it, he swung the hoe back confidently but carelessly. Once the swing was at its apex, Mr. Lee felt the back of his hoe hit something solid. Screams of pain followed. He turned, and to his dismay, he saw Soriya curled up on the dirt, clutching her jaw. Mr. Lee thought he could have broken it. One of the other male teachers came to check out the commotion and upon hearing about the situation said, "Hey, why didn't you pay attention? When you work, you need to pay attention," he scolded.

Then he turned to Soriya and started joking with her.

"Oh no, you're going to be ugly now. Nobody is going to marry you."

Soriya started to wail. Mr. Lee was shocked. Even though she was a nasty person, she still didn't deserve that. The teacher excused Soriya from working for the rest of the day, and he told her to go visit the hospital. Mr. Lee was let off without a warning.

"Man, I was so scared for three days. I thought that it was the end for me," Mr. Lee says.

Mr. Lee hardly had time to see his family. None of his classmates did. After school it was straight to the fields for work. Mr. Lee didn't mind working in the field though as long as he stayed alive, but he would have prefered an easier job. There was one job all the kids yearned for: driving the oxcart into the jungle to collect firewood for the village.

It was the least physically laborious task, but it still required skill. Since there were no paved roads, only uneven dirt ones, a skilled navigator had to guide the oxen away from potholes so the cart would not get stuck. Although all students had a chance to drive the cart, most of them did not do a good job as they would either get stuck in potholes or crash into trees, rendering the vehicle useless. Mr. Lee soon emerged as the only skilled navigator of the group, and he also succeeded at controlling the oxen. The teachers took notice of this because Mr. Lee eventually became the permanent oxcart driver for the school.

The teachers allowed Mr. Lee to bring a friend along on the oxcart to help him collect firewood. As a result, he always asked Samang to go with him. It was likely the easiest job they would ever be assigned in Brave Village because they mostly sat in the cart. Mr. Lee and Samang barely had to move unless it was to collect firewood, and since it didn't take long to collect their daily quotas, they used the extra time to create homemade traps, placing them in hollow openings of dead trees where the rabbits and squirrels would occasionally nest. Every successful score meant extra rations for them and their close friends at the school. Even when Mr. Lee and Samang worked slower, it never took long, leaving at least half of the day open. Although they had the option to stay in the forest longer, Mr. Lee wanted to earn the villagers' respect, so he usually joined his classmates in the fields afterwards. Samang, who preferred to conserve his energy, always disapproved of returning early, but since Mr. Lee could simply choose another classmate to replace him, he was in no position to negotiate.

It was a hot, sunny afternoon when Mr. Lee and Samang were sitting on the ground close to the river having already collected the daily firewood. All of a sudden, the stillness was shattered as they saw two men wading upstream, knee-deep in the muddy water. Both wore frantic looks upon their faces as they hurriedly plunged through the river, almost as if they were being chased. Mr. Lee described the two men as Big Guy and Skinny Guy.

"Are we in Thailand yet?" asked Big Guy.

"I think so," said Skinny Guy. "The Cambodian people speaking here kind of have a Thai accent. Maybe we are right on the border."

Both men noticed Mr. Lee and Samang observing them, and they immediately tried to hide behind bamboo bushes, even ducking their heads underwater. Mr. Lee thought it was odd that there were people in the area because it was work time in the fields. After a while, once the two men were out of sight, the boys were approached by three Khmer Rouge soldiers. They looked like they were on high alert; all three had their machine guns in their hands ready to fire at any moment.

"Have you boys seen two guys anywhere along this river?" one of them asked.

"Yeah," Samang replied, gesturing upstream.

After another 30 minutes, Mr. Lee and Samang were heading back to the school when they began hearing commotion coming from the main village. Following the noise, they discovered the three guards from earlier, only this time, they were accompanied by other armed regiments. Mr. Lee and Samang stood next to the small crowd of villagers, trying to get a closer look at what was happening. In the center of all the commotion was Big Guy and Skinny Guy, still wet from the river, their bare hands and feet tied, their clothes ragged and bloodied. There was a female Khmer Rouge official that looked like she was high in rank. Mr. Lee had never seen her before, likely she travelled around to patrol all the villages in Preah Vihear.

"Where are you from?" she demanded, her arms crossed and face stern.

"A village far away," Big Guy replied.

"Why did you come here then?"

"Well… in my village we are just chickens in a cage. We are taken out one at a time to be slaughtered."

Big Guy didn't flinch from her probing questions. He looked into her eyes and answered as honestly and eloquently as he could. The female Khmer Rouge official signaled the soldiers to whip the two of them, the same whips used on cows and oxen. Both men's skin reddened from the first few lashes, and Mr. Lee saw marks appearing that eventually started to bleed. Despite their injuries, neither of the men screamed. They laid there, curled up on the dirt, taking repeated blows from the cracking whips. Mr. Lee respected their bravery and refusal to project pain. They weren't afraid to die.

Finally, the whipping stopped.

"So, tell me, do you want to live, or do you want to die?" the female soldier asked.

Big Guy speaks up again.

"You know what? I had four kids who were killed. I had a wife that was killed. My family, and my friends all have been killed! I am one of the last alive in my family, and I have nothing left… And you are asking me if I want to live or if I want to die? That's a very simple question to answer. As a human being, you want to live. Who wants to die?" Big Guy paused for a moment to catch his breath before he continued. "A cracked seed that is buried under a ground full of rocks will still try to grow. Everything in this world will struggle to survive."

Skinny Guy lowered his head. Mr. Lee stood there reeling from the impact of his words. He knew at that moment they were going to die, and they knew it too. They decided it was better to die dramatically, but with a clear conscience. When Big Guy ended his soliloquy, the female official gestured to the soldiers to take them deep into the jungle.

The very next afternoon, Mr. Lee and Samang set off for their routine firewood collection. As they ventured deeper into the wilderness, they found Big Guy and Skinny Guy, their limp bodies sprawled on the ground, stained with fresh blood. Their abdomens had several bloody holes where they were punctured by the bamboo spears which lay rotting next to them. They were further mutilated by bite marks, likely from wild animals prowling at night.

"A bullet was worth more than a human life," Mr. Lee says.

That night, Mr. Lee was in the male living quarters on the second floor of the school, talking and laughing with several other boys after a typical day of field work. Others were lounging in their makeshift hammocks or on a sheet on top of the floor getting ready to go to sleep.

Prak walked in with another male teacher. He pointed at four kids including Mr. Lee and instructed them to follow him outside into the cornfield. Mr. Lee had no idea what was going on, but he had to follow orders. Upon reaching the cornfields, they were met with more soldiers, some with guard dogs on leashes.

Mr. Lee heard the loud bang of a bamboo stick hitting a large hollow container, the signal for intruders. "Everyone, separate and search for any suspicious activity," Prak ordered before handing them all a knife. Mr. Lee trekked the maze of the cornfield, peering among dense rows of vegetation for intruders. Not long after beginning his search, Mr. Lee heard a gunshot, and instinctively dropped down to the dirt to avoid any potential bullets. When Prak later found Mr. Lee, he was still on the ground clutching his knife.

"Head back to the school. The adults will handle this," Prak said.

Mr. Lee and the other boys waited for Prak to return, and when he came back with the other soldiers, he explained what had happened. Prak thought he had seen the shadowy figure of the intruder but wasn't sure because it was too dark. The shadow, noticing his presence, began to move. With assistance from a guard dog, Prak was led to a hilltop where he was met by the figure illuminated by the moon. This was enough evidence of an intruder for Prak, prompting him to fire a shot. The intruder tumbled down the cliff. When Prak ran to the top and looked over the edge, the figure was gone, leaving nothing but a trail of blood behind.

Prak followed the blood towards the river where the bridge connecting the school to the village was located, before it abruptly ended, indicating that the intruder had jumped into the river. Returning with backup soldiers, it didn't take long to track down the location of the intruder. When Prak revealed the responsible perpetrator, Mr. Lee recognized the name and couldn't believe it. The shadowy figure who tried to steal corn was Samang's older brother Narith.

The next morning, Mr. Lee told Samang the news, and all Samang did was tremble. Samang expected that his older brother had already been executed, despite the fact that Prak hadn't mentioned what happened after they caught their thief. As usual, after lunch break Mr. Lee and Samang took the oxcart to collect firewood. However, once they arrived in the woods, they hid the oxcart behind some foliage and headed towards the shantytown to see Samang's mother. In case she didn't already know, Samang wanted her to hear the news from him.

Similar to the scene with Big Guy and Skinny Guy, there was a group of people surrounding the side of the shack belonging to Samang's family. Most of the crowd was made up of young village women, all of whom were weeping. Even though Narith was from Phnom Penh, he had managed to win the hearts of many girls in the village due to his looks and involvement with the *chllop*, a special team of post-adolescent teenagers who performed special duties for the village collective. Mr. Lee followed Samang as he desperately pushed through the throng of sobbing fangirls to get to his older brother.

When they reached the front of the crowd, they saw Narith drowning in his own blood. Samang's mother, with tears in her eyes, used every towel she had to apply pressure to the bullet wound on his right arm. Despite her efforts, the blood soaked through all the towels, leaving maroon and muddy cloth in the place of human flesh. He was being interrogated by none other than the same travelling, female Khmer Rouge official who ordered the execution of Big Guy and Skinny Guy. She must be the Grim Reaper because she only appeared when there was the prospect of death.

"Why did you steal the corn?" she asked Narith, interrogating him with that same probing intensity.

"Because I was hungry," Narith said.

"Can you tell me how many people were there helping you last night?"

"Only me."

"Well, since you are injured like this, we have to take you to the hospital."

Narith paused. His resolve seemed weak. His skin grew paler as he kept losing blood.

"I know what that means. You guys are just going to kill me. It's fine though… Just please don't hurt my family. My mom, my little sister, and brother are all that's left. You can execute me in any way… but please… don't hurt my family."

Silence filled the room except for the sobs of his female admirers. Mr. Lee didn't want to look over at Samang. He kept his head down and focused on Narith's blood soaking the earth around him. Mr. Lee couldn't cry. Too many things had made him cry that nothing made him cry anymore. Narith continued.

"Last night after I was shot and chased, I jumped into the river with the intent to kill myself, but I realized that if I was going to die anyway, I would see my mother one last time, and breathe my last breath with her there."

It seemed that when people faced death, they preferred to die on their own terms. Whether it was dying a brave death like Big Guy and Skinny Guy or seeking the comfort of a mother's touch like Narith, their final moments were one of the few things that the Khmer Rouge couldn't own. Shortly after Narith finished speaking, an oxcart came. The soldiers proceeded to take Narith into the jungle, and Samang and Mr. Lee left shortly after.

The next morning Prak walked triumphantly into class with a blood-stained knife in one hand as he began class with an announcement.

"I killed the thief that tried stealing corn from our field."

He raised the knife in his hand at the class.

"Look. The blood is not even completely wiped off," Prak said, and he continued to brag about how he chopped his head off before digging multiple craters in the body with his bamboo spears. Mr. Lee felt his stomach turn with discomfort. He glanced over at Samang who kept a stoic expression on his face.

"Anyone who commits a crime will suffer the consequences. Anyone who stands up to someone who commits a crime will ALSO suffer the consequences." Prak waved his knife at the class. Then he looked at Samang, aware that he was Narith's little brother. Samang's blank expression never changed, but Mr. Lee sensed the rage building up inside of him.

A few months after Narith's death, nothing significant had changed from everyday life at school. Mr. Lee wished he could see his family more but work always kept him busy. Sometimes he would sneak out to visit Guang for a short time before returning to Prak with his daily collection of firewood.

Still, Mr. Lee was never able to see his siblings because they worked in the fields all day or were a part of the *chllop* team.

Prak arrived at class one morning with scratches all across his arms, legs, and face. He told the class that he was attacked by a tiger the day before.

When the class adjourned for lunch, Samang walked with Mr. Lee.

"I was so happy when I heard that news," Samang said. "He only got hurt by a tiger this time, however next time he might not be so lucky."

Mr. Lee laughed and offered him reassurance. Samang had been through a lot of emotional trauma after losing Narith. Seeing him happy made Mr. Lee believe their hell still had its good moments.

Whenever Mr. Lee would navigate the oxcart, he always looked up at the sky in the direction of the palm trees. He saw workers from the village, mostly "old people," climbing all the way to the top, sometimes as high as 60 feet from the ground. They had no harnesses, just the support of makeshift bamboo ladders holding the weight of their feet.

Before Mr. Lee injured his foot, there was a day when he saw a muscular man carrying a bamboo stick with buckets hanging from the edges. As he was walking to the field to start his day with a few of the "old people," Mr. Lee turned around and faced them. "What is that?" Mr. Lee asked.

One of the teenagers walking with him responded.

"Palm juice."

"Can we try?"

"We can ask."

The teenager was kind. He already knew the man selling the palm juice, so he asked him if Mr. Lee could try a sample. The seller, who was sitting down on the grass, smiled and asked Mr. Lee for his bamboo cup.

According to Mr. Lee, he had never in his life drunk something that sweet. He asked the seller where he got this juice, and he pointed to the palm trees in the distance.

"Man, I thought it was so tall, and it looked really scary. But I was young, and I had already been through a lot so I felt like nothing could scare me," Mr. Lee says.

After that day, Mr. Lee constantly thought about those tall palm trees, fantasizing over how it would be like to be at the top. Eventually he convinced himself that he would become a climber so that he could also barter some palm juice. All he needed was an opportunity to learn from someone.

Mr. Lee would receive that opportunity during his tenure at school. He learned that one of the children in his group of "new people" used to climb palm trees for the village before being sent to school. His name was Davuth, and Mr. Lee had luckily already befriended him. Mr. Lee asked if he could teach him how to climb.

"I can't teach you much. The real instructor is up there, at the top of the tree," Davuth said.

Mr. Lee initially had no idea what Davuth meant until he began his climbing lessons. Davuth agreed to teach Mr. Lee the basics if Mr. Lee picked him occasionally to collect firewood. They reached a compromise where Davuth and Samang alternated every other day. Samang was a little disappointed because he was starting to get used to the ease of that job, but he understood that this was something Mr. Lee had wanted for a while.

During the days when Davuth accompanied Mr. Lee, they sneaked off not too far from the heart of the jungle to a small palm tree that had been abandoned by its climbers. Davuth taught him how to squeeze the palm juice from the flower at the top of the tree, how to climb the tree using the bamboo ladder, and how to hold the bucket on the climb up. At first, Mr. Lee wasn't able to squeeze out much juice, and he scaled the tree rather clumsily. However, with time, he slowly improved.

"It's just like cooking man. I used to suck when I first got into the food business, but with a lot of practice I got better at it."

Davuth graduated school a few months after teaching Mr. Lee how to climb. By then, Mr. Lee felt confident that he could do it on his own. Right before he left, Davuth told Mr. Lee to come and find him so that he could recommend him to the leader in charge of the palm tree climbers.

PALM TREES

"**S**ORRY! I FORGOT that I had to wash the dishes before I left," Amanda says, as she hurriedly walks over to where I am sitting at the coffee shop. It is now early November and gone are the long summer sunsets, replaced by brisk winds, falling leaves, and worn cardigans. Although the change in seasons is partly to blame, my conversations with Mr. Lee have drastically lengthened our sessions to the point that I don't return to my dormitory until nightfall. Visiting the Lees has stopped becoming a mere obligation for a school project. Seeing Mrs. Lee smile as she stops to cut her chicken breasts and having Mr. Lee pat me on the back and then ask me about my week makes me feel welcome. I have started to look forward to every interview as if I were meeting to hang out with friends.

"I guess tardiness really does run in your family," I tell Amanda.

We both laugh. Both of us have been busy with our own personal projects, making it difficult to find time to meet. After receiving our coffee, Amanda vents to me about how the long hours of preparing for her first big E-Sports tournament have engulfed her in a constant routine of late nights and headaches, although she remains rather optimistic. She is more animated despite worries that this tournament may be a waste of her time. The conversation then turns towards me.

"My dad and I talk about your interviews the same night it happens. He wonders why you don't laugh at his jokes," she says.

I almost choke on my coffee. I put the cup down.

"It feels disrespectful because he's talking about all these terrible things that happened to him," I say, before clarifing that Mr. Lee is very laid-back and easy-going, and that his jokes are indeed funny. "It's almost surprising that he's been through so much because he doesn't show it."

"Yeah, he was questioning whether or not you had a sense of humor. He jokes around because he doesn't want the mood to always be sad."

I nod but don't respond. Amanda takes a sip of coffee and continues.

"My dad's really excited about this book. He thinks it's gonna be great. That maybe he'll get a movie adaption."

Great, I thought. A movie adaption? Seems a bit too ambitious, so hopefully it's just one of his jokes. Amanda isn't the only one worrying now. In the end, will this book be good enough to meet Mr. Lee's standards, or anyone's for that matter?

"I'll try my best," I say.

During the next interview I ask Mr. Lee about his sense of humor.

First, he laughs. "I hope you like my jokes man. I am trying to make the book a little funny. You know, we don't want it to be sad, sad, sad all the time. It's like a Jackie Chan movie. You got violent fighting then you got a little comedy afterwards. I don't want to go straight to the bad stuff," he says.

Sometime in late 1977 when he was almost 17, Mr. Lee finally "graduated" from school. After almost a year of living in Brave Village, he was deemed old and fit enough to work with the adults again. Mr. Lee planned to move back in with Guang and his siblings in the shantytown and hoped he could surprise his mother upon arrival.

As soon as Mr. Lee settled back in and embraced an overjoyed, tearful Guang, he ventured out to the grassy area where the palm trees were. Now that Mr. Lee was free from the restrictions of school, he could focus on joining the climbers at the tops of the palm trees. First, however, he had to find Davuth.

When he arrived, he saw that there was a significant amount of people either climbing palm trees or resting at the top although there were some "old people" climbers lounging about on the ground. Mr. Lee went and approached them. With his significantly improved Khmer, Mr. Lee asked if they knew where Davuth was. In response, they pointed at a palm tree about 100 meters from where they were sitting, and Mr. Lee could just make out Davuth's figure descending from the top.

Mr. Lee walked over to the tree as Davuth was reaching the ground. Upon seeing Mr. Lee, he loosened his grip and waved.

"Can you still recommend me?" Mr. Lee asked.

"Yes, I can. Wait here, let me find me Kiri," Davuth said.

Davuth returned with a taller, dark-skinned, more muscular Khmer Rouge official.

"Climb to the top of the tree," Kiri said.

Mr. Lee recognized that this was a test of his skill, and he passed it with flying colors. When he climbed down back to the ground, Kiri praised him.

"You will be climbing palm trees from now on," he said.

Not only had Mr. Lee acquired the job he wanted, but now he had status. Being a palm tree climber in the village was coveted as an important, almost professional job.

Once Mr. Lee would reach the top of a tree, he used his knife to cut the palm flower as demonstrated by Davuth. After squeezing it, he would watch as drops of fresh juice flowed out, before replacing the full bucket that had been collecting underneath with the empty one he climbed up with. He would repeat this process by climbing a total of 15 palm trees twice a day, once in the morning and again in the late afternoon. Despite it being a prestigious job, Mr. Lee's schedule was not any less hectic. Kiri monitored him for the first two weeks, refining and scrutinizing his techniques, while also teaching Mr. Lee how to convert palm juice into palm sugar.

Kiri had all the palm tree climbers dig a big hole in the dirt to act as a placeholder for a giant pot, under which a fire would burn. After climbers collected a bucket of palm juice, it would go into the pot until they all met their quotas. The juice would boil in the pot, and climbers had to stir it until it solidified into sugar.

The last thing Kiri taught Mr. Lee was how to build the bamboo ladder used to ascend up the tree. He wore a basket like a backpack with rope straps that carried pieces of chopped bamboo. He had to build as he climbed up by chopping off the ladder legs that he was replacing above him, and then tying on the new legs from his basket. The new legs would last a year until he had to replace it again. If the bamboo limb was centered on the trunk, there would be approximately 6 inches on both sides for his feet.

"I tell a lot of young people this quote from when I climbed palm trees. You could use it too," Mr. Lee says. "When I sliced that flower, palm juice would come out one drop at a time, but at the end of the day, when I get that bucket from the tree in the morning and night… it is full. One drop at a time will eventually make the bucket full. It is the same with money. If you save a little amount of money, at first it does not look like much. After a while though, you will see a lot of money."

I laugh and nod in agreement. I remembered Amanda telling me that he likes handing out life advice in conversations.

Climbing palm trees proved to be a dangerous job. Workplace accidents frequently turned fatal as strong winds provided a multitude of threats. When climbers reached the top of a tree against a strong breeze, they would have to worry about the large branches protruding from the top of the trunk. Since the trunks of palm trees were thinner, a strong enough force would make them sway, causing its branches to thrash around. As Mr. Lee had witnessed, if a climber was on the wrong side of the trunk, that person was flattened and effectively killed by the branches.

Whenever the skies were cloudy, or if he started feeling a strong breeze, Mr. Lee became highly alert. He watched the palm trees from a distance while he scaled to see what direction the wind was blowing, making sure to climb on the side where the wind hit his back. There came a day when the winds really picked up, and Mr. Lee demonstrated his vigor to the other climbers.

The force of the winds was so strong that the upper half of the trunks were bending at a 45-degree angle. None of the climbers dared risk their lives, so they all waited on the ground for the winds to pass. Mr. Lee also tried climbing down, but he was too high up, and the winds made it impossible for him to move. He had no choice but to hold on. Thankfully, Mr. Lee had already calculated the direction the wind was blowing, enabling him to move to the safe side. As the winds continued, his arms hugged the trunk, his legs supported by the bamboo ladder. It was enough to help him hold on. When the winds finally calmed down, Mr. Lee continued to scale to the top of the palm tree even though the bucket waiting for him at the top had been blown off. To celebrate his triumph, he sat down at the top of the tree and took swigs from his own personal palm juice.

"The village folk at the bottom thought I was crazy. You could say I was kind of a daredevil," Mr. Lee says.

Then there was the lightning. During thunderstorms, lightning would occasionally set the palm trees on fire. Mr. Lee recalled a time when he was halfway up a tree and a strike was so close it rang in his ears. Before he knew it, the top of the tree was engulfed in flames, forcing him to scramble back down.

Bees also hid inside the hollow bamboo tubes on the sides of the ladder steps. There were times when Mr. Lee would grab the edge of a bamboo leg as he climbed and then recoil, wincing in pain as the bees stung his palms. Mr. Lee also witnessed one of the climbers fall off the trunk and break his leg after being stung by bees and losing his balance on the ladder. That climber was actually lucky. Usually when climbers fell, they either ended up dead or paralyzed. One man even lost four fingers because he grabbed one of the palm tree's saw-like leaves in order to break his fall.

"Looking back, I can't believe how much I gambled my life every day," Mr. Lee says. "At my age now, I'm a lot more careful."

Mr. Lee harvested more than enough palm juice and made enough sugar to meet the quotas, and along the way, he learned a recipe that utilized his extra juice in a way that would forever transform his life in Preah Vihear.

"I made this thing called sour palm juice. The people in the village called it *athuy*. Everyone loved it because it was the only drink in the village that made you drunk."

Mr. Lee learned the trade from one of the tree climbers who also sold *athuy*. First, he had to ferment the palm juice in a container with special tree bark and roots. He would leave small canisters at the tops of his assigned palm trees or in a large cement container where the juice would soak under the sun for a few days.

Mr. Lee quickly earned the trust of the village higher-ups because, according to him, they LOVED to drink. "When they got a hold of my drink, they got hooked, man. It's like drugs, you get hooked," he says. Even the soldiers acted warmer towards Mr. Lee.

After a long day of working, the village leaders would seek the climbers that sold *athuy* and ask if they had any. Sometimes they even asked first thing in the morning. In exchange, Mr. Lee received extra rations.

Mr. Lee and the other *athuy* dealers were also popular at parties and weddings. Nobody in the village (except the important people it seemed) could drink alcohol unless it was a special occasion. Mr. Lee felt it was unfair treatment towards the "new people" because it further marginalized them. He decided then to offer *athuy* to them for nothing in exchange as they walked to work.

"Now I wouldn't let them have too much because then they'd get too drunk," Mr. Lee says, as he chuckles. "I'd say if you were not used to drinking, then 16 ounces of my *athuy* would give you a buzz."

Mr. Lee then starts going off on a tangent about the health benefits of *athuy*. "It's actually pretty healthy unless you abuse it, because every time you drink it, your pee comes out clearer compared to when you would drink beer... Like straight pure, no bubbles... just straight pure. That means it cleans up your body you know."

Mr. Lee sought to maximize his business by garnering more free time during the day. If there was adequate light from the moon and stars, he would start work in the middle of the night while all the other climbers were still asleep. Once everyone was awake, Mr. Lee was already done for the day. Then he would sleep for a little bit, make some *athuy*, and then trade it for more food.

"So did your village have a killing field?" I ask.

"They usually took people into the jungle to execute them, but if they killed you, then they would eat you," Mr. Lee says.

I lean forward in my seat. "What?!" I had not read anything about cannibalism during my prior research.

"Sometimes they wouldn't eat the whole body, but the liver and heart were the most important things to my village. I will tell you about some of it now," Mr. Lee said.

Since Mr. Lee left school, he moved back in with his family at the shantytown. However, Grandma Guang had been so coveted by the village that shortly after Mr. Lee returned, she was granted her own small one-room wooden house as a testament to her importance. Mr. Lee was the only person throughout the day who could keep Guang and the babies in some company.

One afternoon while Mr. Lee was resting on the wooden floor, a menacing looking man appeared at the entrance. He had an old Chinese Type 56 assault rifle strapped around his shirtless body. His eyes were bloodshot red with a touch of purple, and his face was a shade of plum and jade which may have been from primal makeup. He was holding a bag of dried fish. When he saw Grandma Guang sitting quietly and watching over all the sleeping babies, his expression softened.

"Did my princess give you any trouble today?" the man asked.

"Not at all Teen, she slept all morning," Guang replied. They had a brief conversation before Guang handed Teen his daughter. Then he handed her the dried fish as a gift before leaving.

She later explained to Mr. Lee that the menacing man named Teen had recently been assigned to Brave Village from the neighboring Perseverance Village after a merger was issued between the two towns. Guang didn't know much, but she had heard rumors that Teen was a ruthless pit bull that prowled around his old village. However, from the few interactions she had had with him and his daughter, he seemed kind.

Close to sunset, Mr. Lee and the other climbers would sit and drink under the palm trees to end the workday. Normally, socializing in small groups or engaging in flirtatious activity could be punishable by death, but climbers were somehow excused. In fact, they were joined by village leaders, their friends, and family members. Mr. Lee learned a lot about the gruesome practices of the people oppressing him through stories they would tell under the influence of *athuy*. In fact, village leaders were proud of their cruelty, often boasting or debating each other over whose murder was more graphic.

In the beginning Mr. Lee wouldn't dare say anything. He was always on edge because the village leaders became drunk fast and sometimes would start glaring at him, suspicion etched upon their faces. Mr. Lee simply provided the *athuy* and listened with a blank expression, masking his fear and disgust.   "For a while, I couldn't sleep at night," Mr. Lee says.

After his first encounter with Teen, a few days passed until he heard the name mentioned under the palm trees, this time in a much more barbaric way.

"We suspected that this family of thirteen had black magic properties," one of the village leaders said. "Teen led a group of us to their home so that we could deal with those troublemakers."

When the group of murderers were assembled in front of the house, they interrogated the family about their black magic. Teen decided their answer wasn't sufficient and took the lead inciting the massacre.

"He killed the youngest child first, and then started targeting the other children," the leader said. Instead of his gun, Teen impaled them with a sharpened bamboo stick. Everyone else followed his lead with their own spears and garden tools. The last person still alive was a young adult man. He had been beaten and stabbed multiple times already but was still conscious. Teen walked up to where he laid and stood right in front of him, his body wracked and riddled with wounds.

"Why didn't you use your black magic powers to kill us? Or to protect your family?" Teen demanded.

"If I protected them today, could I have protected them tomorrow, or the day after, and the days after that?" the man replied. He then explained to Teen that he was immortal, and the only way they could kill him and stop his black magic was for them to bring a virgin woman to urinate on his body.

Mr. Lee laughs as he recounts the story. "I don't know how true that is, but the way those leaders were talking, it seemed legit."

Another leader in the palm tree circle confirmed the story by telling everyone that his daughter fulfilled the man's request. She took off all her clothes, stood over him, and peed directly on his body, thus relieving him of his powers so Teen could finish him off.

Mr. Lee and Davuth were on a delivery run with bamboo canisters of *athuy*. Earlier they had been called by a village leader for an order of the drink. He told them to meet him at the rice fields at sunset, and they would be paid with quality rations.

As they approached the fields, they saw several torchlights illuminated in the distance accompanied by raucous voices. Quickly looking around for a place to hide, they spotted the barn that stored all of the village's rice production. It was close enough to the torches that they could see and hear what was going on without detection.

"As a true communist person, if I have done something wrong, I do not need to be criticized... I will take my own life right now."

The voice was undoubtedly Teen's, and as Mr. Lee watched from the barn window, he saw Teen standing up and facing other Khmer Rouge village leaders, a revolver in his hand. Guards surrounded them, their torches bathing the scene in light. Teen aimed the gun at his forehead, but before he could pull the trigger, his father screamed and ran towards him.

"Are you crazy!" his dad cried, pulling the gun away from his son's face. Mr. Lee assumed all the commotion came from the other village leaders complaining about Teen. He would later find out they accused Teen of killing people without consulting them first.

At this point in the story, Mr. Lee is crouching on top of his plastic chair. His Nike slides are on top of the seat. His voice had gotten progressively louder, which happens every time he is excited about something. I have a feeling that Teen, a brutal, murderous, Khmer Rouge leader, had a real impact, whether good or bad, on Mr. Lee's life.

One day, on Guang's request, Mr. Lee headed to Teen's house to pick something up. Mr. Lee arrived at a modest-looking wooden house and was greeted by Teen's wife who welcomed him inside where he was overwhelmed by Teen's collection of meats and pelts. Mr. Lee was led outside and saw some of the flesh from his collection hanging and cooking over a burning stove. The greases were dripping onto the fire making the flames rise and dance. Mr. Lee was confused. What kind of meat was that? He had not recognized it before in the jungle or in the markets of Phnom Penh. Teen's wife gave Mr. Lee the package for Guang, and he took the opportunity to ask about the meats that were cooking.

"Oh. My husband... I think he killed another human being," she replied.

There could only be one reason why Teen was letting human meat cook over a fire, and nausea overcame Mr. Lee.

Teen already had a reputation for being ruthless, but did he go as far as eating the people he killed, too? Mr. Lee would return to Teen's house occasionally per request from Guang, and there would always be hearts and livers around the house. However, Mr. Lee's suspicions about Teen were not confirmed until several weeks later.

The son of one of Teen's friends, Sovann, joined their social circle one night, and as usual, the village leaders and other important people shared gossip for the day while the climbers listened. At one point, the conversation focused on Teen, which prompted Sovann to speak up. He said that one time he was headed into the jungle to execute an agitator with a group of Khmer Rouge soldiers, his father, and Teen. Sovann, who was a part of the *chllop* team, was holding the man at gunpoint while the other soldiers around him forced him to walk forward. They kept going until the group found a tree trunk small enough for the guilty man to hug all the way around with his arms. Once this was accomplished, Teen and his friend tied the man's hands together. Teen then grabbed a short axe from his toolbelt, and sliced straight down into the man's nape. He stuck his finger inside and pulled the spine out. Afterwards, the person's heart and liver was shared with the entire group, washed down with some palm juice. Mr. Lee would later learn that such acts stemmed from animist beliefs that the human liver housed bravery and courage in a person.

Should someone eat the liver of a slain enemy, it was believed that the stored courage and bravery would transfer over to the eater. Perhaps eating other human body parts was attributed to that same philosophy, or perhaps Teen simply salivated at the act. Mr. Lee was lucky that Grandma Guang took such good care of Teen's daughter because if the Lees were ever on his bad side, they might have ended up over that fire.

FINDING A HOME

ONE OF THE first questions I ever asked Mrs. Lee was whether or not they sold Cambodian food. "We used to, but we took it off the menu because it didn't sell well," she said.

During the interviews, I asked Mr. Lee the same question while we were on one of our tangents. "Nah man. It doesn't sell... But to be honest, I don't like Cambodian food that much. I prefer Vietnamese and Chinese."

Since the Lees lived in a Chinese household, they mainly ate their native food. Despite their preferences, Cambodian food was the means for survival. They weren't worried about flavor or creativity; they wanted something that could fill their bellies and give them the strength to live another day. After returning home from an interview, however, Amanda texted me saying that Mrs. Lee forgot to hand me a Cambodian dish she prepared, and that I should come by sometime for it. The next day, I returned to Oriental Kitchen a few minutes after opening.

I ring the bell and Mrs. Lee appears.

"Hi Mrs. Lee. Amanda told me you made some Cambodian food for me?"

"Yes, Kenny, hold on a minute."

She comes back with everything tightly wrapped in a plastic bag. I pull out my credit card, and as usual, she refuses to charge me.

"Please let me pay for this."

"No, don't pay. It's my pleasure," she says. "It's called *prahok*. Eat the paste with the lemon juice. It's really good," Mrs. Lee says.

I return home and place the to-go box in the microwave to heat up the leftovers. When I open the box, a strong fishy odor penetrates the air. *Prahok* is crushed fish paste, usually mudfish, but Mrs. Lee explained that she had to substitute the mudfish with shrimp paste. It looks like gray ground beef with traces of orange—probably carrots. Although the meal appears less than appetizing, my philosophy on food is to taste it before making a judgement, so I dump the oyster pail full of rice in the *prahok* and mix it together. Then I take my first bite, finding that it tastes like a better version of tuna. With the hot rice mixed in, the flavor balances while also adding texture.

For my second bite I open a sauce cup of lemon juice and dip a spoonful of *prahok* and rice into it. Mrs. Lee was right. It may not seem like it, but the rich acidic sourness of the lemon juice is the perfect complement to the slightly sweet and fishy, tuna-like paste. This meal feels special. It is thoughtful. It is uniquely Cambodian.

The quality of life for Mr. Lee steadily improved once he became a climber. The more *athuy* he produced, the more chicken, wild vegetables, and rice he received in exchange. When coupled with edible gifts Guang received from important leaders like Teen, Mr. Lee had enough to distribute evenly with the rest of the family. Mr. Lee was still feeling hungry most of the time, but it wasn't enough to keep him from working. It helped that Kiri was also a rather kind and flexible boss; as long as the palm juice quotas were met, there was no need to work anymore. He also didn't care when the climbers started or finished, even praising people like Mr. Lee at climber meetings for waking up before sunrise to start working.

As Mr. Lee grew comfortable with his new schedule, he received some unexpected news, and he had a tough decision to make. Teen had visited Guang and told her that he was being recalled back to his home in Perseverance Village. Since Teen loved her so much as the caregiver of his daughter, he insisted to his superiors that Grandma Guang must move with him. The kids were allowed to accompany her as well. For Teng, Seng, Chang, Bieng, and Guah it was a no-brainer to stick together, but for Mr. Lee it was more complicated.

Although he remembered his father's advice to stick together, he had a comfortable life as a climber in Brave Village. He was not guaranteed that he would have the same opportunity if he left. It would also mean less food for the family, something worth more than staying together. He insisted to Teen that he wanted to stay and work in Brave Village, which upset the rest of his family. However, they understood that staying put gave everyone a better chance to survive, and Perseverance Village wasn't more than a couple of miles walking distance.

Teen told Mr. Lee that he would not be able to stay in the wooden house and that he had to find another home. Under the palm trees the following day, he told everyone around him that he needed a new place to stay. One of the few "new people" climbers offered his shack to him. Once his family moved out, Mr. Lee grabbed his spoon and hammock from the now-empty wooden house and moved back into the shantytown.

Mr. Lee didn't last long in his new home. The climber who invited him had a spot outside the shack where he sat and smoked tobacco, so he always kept to himself. Like a statue, he seldom moved a muscle and constantly stared off into the distance, speaking only to yell at his daughter for being too loud. His wife was always lying down on an old blanket, moaning from some unidentifiable pain.

"There are no doctors. Nobody can help her," he said.

Mr. Lee eventually felt like a burden staying with them. Since he didn't provide anything of value that could help the family, he decided that it would be better if he left.

A village leader who oversaw some of the field work, and a regular *athuy* user, offered him his home next. This new house Mr. Lee stayed in was nicer; however the leader frequently yelled at Mr. Lee for having his friends over, saying that they made too much noise. It wasn't long until one evening Mr. Lee was kicked out of the house.

That same night, Mr. Lee lingered at town hall, taking his time finishing his dinner. He was the last person still there when the head chef of the village approached him.

"Why haven't you left yet?" she asked.

Mr. Lee explained all the events that had happened from Teen leaving with Guang and his siblings, to him wanting to stay and climb, and how his past two living situations had not been ideal. "Is it fine if I sleep on the table tonight? I have no place to go," Mr. Lee said.

"Nonsense," said the head chef. She offered him to stay with her family.

She led Mr. Lee to one of the nicest buildings in the entire village. It was a large two-floor wooden house with mahogany floors. The roof was made of a thin material that looked like bricks. Meeting the family inside, Mr. Lee realized that he was living with two of his regulars under the palm trees (*athuy* really expanded his connections), the chef's husband who was a high-ranking village leader, and one of their five sons, Pot.

The chef gave Mr. Lee a bowl of fresh corn which was left over from the town hall, and he went outside and sat on the steps with Pot. As they ate together, Mr. Lee found Pot to be quite peculiar. The perception around the village was that he was a strange child who kept to himself, but Mr. Lee soon discovered that he was an open book. Pot shocked Mr. Lee after he claimed that he was somehow the father-in-law of his own father, and because of that, he was partially shunned by the village. Whether or not that was true, Mr. Lee found himself to be extra wary around him.

The longer Mr. Lee lived with the head chef, the more he noticed Pot's disrespect towards his father. He would often talk back, and sometimes even shout at him, fully believing that he was the superior. Since the verbal abuses didn't happen all too frequently, it was bearable to live with them when compared to the first two families.

Eventually, Pot would get married. A few days before the wedding, his bride-to-be arrived at the house from her village with an oxcart caravan full of her belongings. All the established Brave Village elites owned a large plot of land because everyone's houses were well spread out from each other, quite the opposite from the dozens of hastily built shacks that housed the migrated city people. Since Pot's family was one of the lucky ones, the wedding was held in their backyard, and almost everyone important to the village was there, including Mr. Lee who helped provide all the guests with *athuy*. Pot's father was nowhere to be found during the wedding. He sat inside and drank with a few of his friends.

Mr. Lee used to sleep on the same mat with Pot, but now that he was married, it became improper. As a result, Mr. Lee slept outside on his hammock under the poles that supported their house. The head chef begged Mr. Lee to sleep upstairs with her and her husband, but Mr. Lee said that it was fine, and that he would look for yet another place to stay.

The fourth family that Mr. Lee stayed with would be the last before reuniting with his own family. Mr. Lee was lounging by the stream when he found Maly. She was one of

Chang's best friends, and when their eyes met, she instantly recognized him. After a brief conversation, he asked Maly if she had space to take him in, and within a couple of hours, Mr. Lee had settled into his new home with her two younger brothers Veha and Nhean. Maly and her brothers were from the southern coastal city of Kampot, and when they arrived at Brave Village, they had been orphaned and lost two of their siblings. Maly met Mr. Lee's older sister Chang while working on the fields, and the two had been close friends ever since.

Veha was the second oldest of the three, and he was always in a bad state, deathly thin, and constantly fighting some form of disease. He laid in a corner of the shack by himself suffering from malaria while Maly would take care of him after returning from the fields. Nhean, the younger brother, was one of the most resourceful people Mr. Lee knew. He wasn't a physically imposing person as he stood at a height that resembled Mr. Lee's at 10 years old, but Nhean made up for it with his cunning survival skills. Because of Maly, Mr. Lee, and Nhean's efforts, the four of them never ran out of food.

Early at dawn or late at night, Nhean would go fishing and make animal traps to catch wild chickens and rabbits. Sometimes Mr. Lee would join him since he had experience with traps from his time at school, and Nhean would help refine his techniques. They would bring back their spoils to

Maly who cooked for everyone. Nhean also made knick-knacks like bamboo cups that he would trade for food or cigarettes. Other than the looming fear that Veha could die at any minute from malaria, they lived comfortably together for months. Mr. Lee considered them a second family.

After spending more time climbing and working with Davuth, he eventually introduced Mr. Lee to his father, Phal. Phal had repaired watches in Phnom Penh, and it proved to be a useful trade in the village. Most Khmer Rouge soldiers were rural people, and had never seen watches until they confiscated them from the "new people." All of a sudden, almost all soldiers wore stolen watches. Mr. Lee described it as the most precious item they had ever seen, comparable to diamond rings in developed countries. "Yeah, the way they talk about it, the way they look at it. They always wear it man. Watches to them are kind of like how Americans show off their new car, or their iPhone… Samsung," says Mr. Lee.

Since all the soldiers worked or oversaw the village outside, they would sometimes get rained on. Water would leak into their watches and stop them from functioning correctly. This was where Phal became useful. Soldiers found out that he used to fix watches and forced him to fix theirs since they didn't want their prized treasures to stop working. Similar to Guang, the success and importance of his trade earned him respect within the village; Phal was paid well in chicken meat, dried fish, and vegetables. Communism was explained as one family, one heart, one mind, and one body, but Mr. Lee felt these soldiers kept an abundance of resources while the majority of the village was starving. That didn't seem very equal.

Phal was very greedy. Mr. Lee often visited him with Davuth, and he never offered food when he clearly had a surplus. He even had food like packaged cookies that Mr. Lee had not seen in years.

"His dad was so stingy. I was so hungry, man. Every time I went to their house. Even though I was his son's best friend, I never got any food. I didn't think about it like that until I came to America. Sometimes I lay down in my bed, trying to recall those old memories, and man I didn't understand why people did that. He had all of this stuff, and he didn't want to share any of it. Even though we were considered friends..."

Mr. Lee swore that he would not be like Phal. He makes it a point in his life today to be a giver.

At first when Mr. Lee visited Perseverance Village, he'd bring extra food rations as promised, but the amount wasn't enough. Meals at town hall hardly alleviated his hunger, so Mr. Lee ate some of his rations as well as shared portions with the people he lived with. It wasn't until he hunted with Nhean that Mr. Lee was able to save more food for his family.

Guang only received extra food rations as gratuity (usually from Teen) for her babysitting, so meals were inconsistent. During Mr. Lee's first few visits, his brother Seng had fallen severely ill. His entire body was swollen up like a water balloon, almost twice his normal size. Guang desperately had been asking for advice from the other villagers, and they advised her to feed him more sugar and less salt. She started going to town hall to ask if she could have more sugar, but usually she came home empty-handed. Seng was two years older than Mr. Lee, but he cried like a baby.

Seng's condition continued to worsen, and the soldiers began to notice that he hadn't been working. They said he had to leave for treatment at the Siem Reap hospital. Guang cried as she told Mr. Lee that Seng had been taken away by oxcart. Adequate medical care didn't exist in Democratic Kampuchea; in fact, the only medicine Mr. Lee ever saw in the village other than the incident with Dara was what the villagers called "rabbit dung," tree bark mixed with honey that was boiled and then kneaded into a round black ball. It looked like rabbit feces and it was supposed to be a cure-all for diseases. If someone was sick, they would get a handful of "rabbit dung." Mr. Lee knew there was no guarantee that Seng would ever come back.

Another problem that arose from malnutrition was night blindness, a difficulty seeing in dimly lit environments. It came in spurts. If one person caught it, a mini epidemic would occur. In the villages it was called "chicken eyes." Every time a spike would occur, Khmer Rouge soldiers suspected that some people were faking to excuse themselves from working, so the soldiers devised a test.

A Khmer Rouge soldier would have the suspect hold on to one side with a garden hoe while the soldier held the other end. The soldier then would guide the suspect into the jungle by tugging him from his end of the hoe. He would tell the suspect to follow the direction of his pull. Once they reached a specific spot in the jungle the suspect would have a pothole or a rock obstructing his or her path and the task was to walk straight towards the obstruction. If the suspect stepped and tripped on the pothole or stepped on the rock, the suspect would pass as blind. If the suspect avoided the trap, it would mean death because it proved the suspect was lying.

Under the palm trees, Mr. Lee heard a story that a villager from the shantytown claimed that he had "chicken eyes." The leader who was telling the story apparently unsheathed his knife, made eye contact, and thrusted the knife about one inch from the person's face. The victim blinked, and the leader finished his story by saying that the victim was taken away into the jungle because it was proven that he lied about being blind.

One of the rare moments of freedom and happiness in the village collective and the rest of Preah Vihear was during the three days of the Cambodian New Year.

"For those three days, you are free. That's pretty cool, ain't it? Those three days are the happiest days of the year," says Mr. Lee.

The New Year marked the end of the harvest season, and it was met with rest and celebrations for the next three days, making people forget they were living in hard times. The celebration would start with people spraying water at each other followed by traditional singing and dancing. There was a morning meeting at the town hall where leaders would talk about how everyone could change as a community and how they should strive to chase out the enemies of the Democratic

Kampuchea and work together for the benefit of the country. For once, these meetings provided optimism for the future.

During those three days there would always be plenty to eat. The women in the kitchen would work hard to always have a streamline of food available at town hall. It wasn't the typical rations either. The village killed cows, pigs, and chickens for meat. One popular meal they made was *banh chao*, a Vietnamese dish consisting of crepe with meat tucked inside. There were also noodles and even sweet balls with mung beans for dessert. If Mr. Lee was ever hungry during those three days, he would walk to town hall to get some food. After a hearty meal, people sported jolly moods as they walked around with full bellies, singing and laughing.

Since it was tradition during the New Year to return home to your family, those who were lucky to relieve themselves from their duties for a few days would come visit, and Brave Village became very crowded. Mr. Lee didn't participate much in those festivities. He just enjoyed the rest and the food, except when he was needed to fulfill a higher demand of *athuy* requests. In total, Mr. Lee celebrated three Cambodian New Years in Preah Vihear, and he always made the most of being able to eat as much as he could.

Everyone in the village looked forward to those three days. People talked about how if they were to die, that hopefully it would be after the New Year.

"Those three days were so nice. They made you think you won't have to work 16 hours a day. That you maybe only had to work five or six days a week instead of seven. You felt happy for once. But then the three days pass… game over, man. Go back to your miserable life," Mr. Lee says.

The hopeful attitude brought about by New Year's festivities did nothing to change the harsh conditions of Brave Village. One day, Teen visited to hold a morning meeting before the workday started. Everyone, including the village leaders, was sitting down at the long tables in the dining hall or on the floor. Teen led the meeting on the routine topic about the month's production yields. Everything seemed normal until one of the leaders stood up and started talking animatedly.

"We do not need people who can't produce a benefit for our community. Our village. We don't need people who were born with sickness or disease, because they would be extra weight on this earth," he said.

Mr. Lee was caught off-guard. How could you say that about humans? There weren't any mentally or physically handicapped people in Preah Vihear. Was that the reason? If soldiers weren't satisfied with someone's work, would they just tie that person up with rope and execute them in the jungle? Production and efficiency being the core principles in the village was dehumanizing. This regime was anything but human, but Mr. Lee already knew that. That leader just reaffirmed it.

CHLLOP TEAM

MIDWAY THROUGH 1978, an 18-year-old Mr. Lee had climbed palm trees full time for over half a year and was yearning for change. He talked to Davuth about joining the *chllop* team: a special child task force assembled by the leaders of Brave, Perseverance, and Victory villages. They worked on projects that benefited all three villages such as constructing dams, visiting other areas of Democratic Kampuchea, and helping out with farming on the fields. Nhean, Maly, Veha, Samang and all of Mr. Lee's siblings worked in groups that stayed within their villages called the *krom sruoch*. However, Mr. Lee and Davuth were lucky to avoid working on the *krom sruoch* so far because they were skilled climbers.

It seemed like an immense risk to join the *chllop* team, especially since they had already built comfortable lives climbing palm trees. However, thanks to constant pressure from Davuth, they eventually enlisted together.

For housing, the *chllop* team was separated based on the two sexes and were spread out in shacks in the jungle and the village. Since Mr. Lee was assigned to the latter, he slept in a hammock tied on both ends of bamboo poles that supported the straw roof over his head. Similar to Mosquito Village, there were no walls protecting him from the elements.

Mr. Lee's first ever assignment was to make the tools he would use for work on a local dam. He, along with Davuth and the other new recruits, went into the jungle to look for some bamboo. He found, cut, and brought back to camp two sturdy bamboo sticks. He used them to carry buckets of water or dirt on his back by resting the middle of the pole on the nape of his neck with the two buckets supported on both ends. Mr. Lee used his knife to smooth out the edges and placed the finished product next to him on the dirt. Then he rolled up some tobacco and started chatting with the other new *chllop* members.

While Mr. Lee was distracted, someone snuck up and stole his bamboo poles. When Mr. Lee finally realized they were gone, he spotted a sleeping Chinese giant on the ground, Mr. Lee's poles nestled beside him. Frustrated, Mr. Lee quietly took back his sticks and rejoined the conversation. As he got comfortable, one of the *chllop* members from his hammock yelled at Mr. Lee to watch out behind him.

Mr. Lee turned around and was met with a foot hurtling towards his face. He managed to dodge it before reaching for his knife.

"You stupid ass! If I land a hit on you, you will lay on the ground for the rest of your life," screamed the thief.

"You may lose a foot if you try that again," responded Mr. Lee.

The two froze in time, glaring at each other for several moments. Mr. Lee was on the ground squatting, gripping his knife ready to strike before the thief eventually gave up and walked away.

The following night a fight broke out in the jungle camp between two of the boys. Mr. Lee recognized one as Kong, a former climber. However, unlike Mr. Lee, Kong was forced into the *chllop* team. As a big, stocky dark-skinned Khmer who lived in the village all his life, Kong easily overpowered his opponent, a much smaller boy who didn't look older than 13. After grappling for a minute, Kong managed to pin him down on the dirt before pummeling him with his fists, while the smaller boy tried to cover himself up with his forearms.

"You are too small for me to fight," Kong said.

The smaller boy waited for an opportunity to fight back, and upon noticing a slight opening between Kong's arms, grabbed a piece of plank wood that was next to him and whacked Kong right on the middle of his forehead. The punches ceased. Kong fell to his side, his face a leaking fire-hydrant of blood. There was silence amongst all the boys until it was broken by their group leader rushing over to scold them for the commotion.

"What the hell is going on here?" she asked.

All the boys who witnessed the fight told the truth because nobody wanted to risk facing the wrath of *Angka*. Kong was never mentally the same after receiving that blow, and he was dismissed from the *chllop* team shortly after the incident.

The work Mr. Lee was doing for the *chllop* team was grueling. It was a similar schedule to the field work Mr. Lee used to do before he went to the school. They started from sunrise— without breakfast—to sunset. There was a 15-minute break for lunch, and then dinner at night (if there was food available). They did fieldwork like harvesting rice, but they also helped with other tasks like building a dam. Since the Democratic Kampuchea abolished paper currency, the country's primary source of income for trade was in agricultural yields, mainly rice. The Khmer Rouge sought to increase production through deforestation for arable land, and large-scale irrigation projects like the building of dams and canals. To the village's credit, there was an increase in agricultural yields, but somehow Mr. Lee sometimes received only a bowl of water for lunch.

"They didn't care about us," Mr. Lee says. "Sometimes the barn where they stored the grain was 70-80% full. It was a lot of grain, but where did it go?"

The *chllop* team worked with the *krom sruoch* on a two-week long mission to the outskirts of Preah Vihear. Mr. Lee was left behind as one of the few remaining teen workers to watch over the crops in Brave Village. He was allowed to choose two others to stay behind with him. In his mind, he had to protect the ones he saw were the most vulnerable. First, he picked Samang who was never the same mentally and emotionally after Narith's death; he used to be talkative and full of life, now he stayed mostly silent and still, pent up with resentment. The second person he picked was Veha. He had slowly been recovering from malaria, and according to Maly had only been able to handle light-duty jobs. A lot of the local workers bullied him and even called for him to be killed because he wasn't being productive enough. The three of them were given provisions that would last them two weeks, and they were stationed at a small shack in the middle of the rice field.

The job itself was relaxing and low stress. All they had to do was make sure that animals didn't destroy or eat the crops. If there were no wild animals, there would be no work. However, they were not always this fortunate, as wild cats and snakes frequently made appearances. Therefore, the three of them took rounds walking around the crops, hitting a bamboo stick on rusty metal buckets to scare the animals away. At night they built bonfires and walked the dogs around the fields. Although buffalos proved to be the most frequent visitor, boars were what caused the three boys to fear for their lives. It was never only one boar. The whole family came in packs; there were small boars, their parents, and the really large 300 pound ones that were probably their grandparents. They didn't come as often as the buffalo, but carelessness would lead to a great loss of rice. They were also very aggressive towards humans.

One day, Mr. Lee told Veha and Samang that he planned on climbing one of his palm trees for some fresh juice while the other two went to a nearby stream to fish. Wanting a large supply of juice for later in the afternoon, Mr. Lee decided to begin climbing at sunrise. Even though Mr. Lee spent most of his time with the *chllop* team, he still climbed palm trees on the side, although it was rare because he would often be too tired after a long day working. Once Mr. Lee reached the top of the tree in time to watch the sunrise, he sliced a flower on the palm tree allowing drops of fresh palm juice to drip into his metal bucket. It was a tranquil morning.

Suddenly, screams in the distance pierced the silence. Mr. Lee scanned his surroundings on the ground to pinpoint the noise. Below, workers on the fields were running for their lives because a stray wild boar was chasing them. Mr. Lee then noticed that the boar was heading in the direction of the stream! His eyes frantically searched the area to locate where Veha and Samang were and found that they were approaching the stream from the other direction of the boar. Veha was holding a bucket, and Samang the net, in the direct path of the raging boar. Using all the force from his vocal cords, Mr. Lee tried to warn them but was too late. The boar had already locked its eyes on Veha and charged at him. Veha tried to shield himself from the boar with his bucket, but ultimately failed. He flew back six or seven feet and fell flat on the ground. The bucket flew from his hands. Mr. Lee continued to scream from the sky.

"VEHA GET UP! GET UP AND RUN!"

The boar continued to maul Veha with its tusks. Samang, who had stood frozen in shock, finally dropped the fishing net he was clutching and ran the other way for the nearest tree he could climb. The boar then started to bite Veha, and even from the sky Mr. Lee could see a stream of scarlet flowing. Every time Veha tried to crawl away, the boar charged at him again and knocked him down.

"VEHA COME ON. GET UP!" Mr. Lee screamed.

Eventually, Veha's body gave up and he stopped moving. Mr. Lee thought he was dead. There was no way his fragile body could handle all that damage. The boar seemed to agree because its eyes locked on Samang who had just managed to scale a tree.

Samang was holding on, petrified. The boar ran to him and then tried its hardest to stick his head out to bite him. Samang's posterior was probably only two inches from its tusks. The tree was so small and skinny that it kept swinging Samang around, yet it managed to hold him without breaking. Eventually the boar gave up and retreated into the wilderness.

Mr. Lee rushed down the ladder of the palm tree and ran to Veha's limp body.

"Veha, Veha, are you ok?" Mr. Lee asked.

"Yeah…" he was half-conscious but still alive. However, he was losing too much blood. Mr. Lee saw holes in his breast area where he could see lungs still pumping in his body cavity. Mr. Lee then took off the *krama* around his neck and tied it around Veha's chest to attempt to stop the bleeding.

Two young nurses ran to the scene, and even though Mr. Lee knew they were worthless in this situation, he had no choice but to ask for help.

"Ma'ams please help us! My friend was gouged by that wild boar."

The nurses looked petrified when they saw Veha laying in a pool of his own blood. One of them exclaimed, "Noooo! I'm scared of blood!" before both fled the scene.

"What the hell! You guys are the nurses!" Mr. Lee yelled.

Another tall figure ran towards Mr. Lee, and as he got closer Mr. Lee noticed that it was Chea, another member of the *chllop* team. The only memory Mr. Lee had of Chea was of one incident on the field.

Chea and Mr. Lee had both been assigned by their teams to till the soil. Chea, who belonged to the *chllop* team of another village, was a large and muscular man. His darker complexion was a safe assumption that he was one of the "old people." Chea appeared to be a hard worker because he tilled the soil faster than anyone in their group. At one point, there was a clunking sound after Mr. Lee swung his hoe. Mr. Lee thought he had hit a rock, but when he looked down at what he struck, he saw the back of Chea's head. Chea was passed out, face first in the mud for a few seconds. When he began to stir, he started to rub the spot where Mr. Lee had hit him. He looked at Mr. Lee, and similar to the incident at school with Soriya, Mr. Lee thought his life was over.

However, Chea was the definition of a gentle giant. He merely laughed and said, "man that hurt." He wasn't a killer, but every so often Mr. Lee would see him ordered around to bully people because of his big stature.

"Brother Chea! Please help!" Mr. Lee was in a panic but was relieved to see him. Chea saw the state Veha was in and immediately ran off to a nearby palm tree. He took out his knife and sliced off the rope that held the bamboo steps on the palm tree ladder. He cut the rope of two bamboo legs and ran back to where Mr. Lee and Veha were waiting. Samang, who had since joined them, was ordered by Chea to hand over his *krama*. Chea used Samang's *krama* as well as his own to make a stretcher with the two bamboo poles which they used to carry Veha.

According to Mr. Lee, Chea was at least 240 pounds of muscle. He alone carried one side of the stretcher with ease while Mr. Lee and Samang each carried a pole on the other side. Even with the two of them holding one side, it was hard keeping up with Chea because he moved so swiftly.

The three of them reached the main dirt road where vehicles occasionally passed through. The *kramas* holding Veha were soaked with blood, dripping so fast from the hammock that it left a trail. Off in the distance, an army truck was approaching. Chea instructed Mr. Lee and Samang to put the hammock down, and as soon as it hit the ground, Chea scooped Veha up into his arms. Chea carried Veha to the middle of the dirt road, blocking the truck's path and forcing it to stop. The driver poked his head out of the window.

"What's going on?" he asked.

"This guy needs to get to the hospital," Chea said.

"Well, the hospital is in the direction I am going right now, so get on!"

Chea climbed onto the back of the truck, Veha resting on his lap. Chea took off his shirt and wrapped it around the wounds of Veha's back. As the truck began to move again, Chea held Veha down with his arms to prevent him from moving as they bounced along the uneven dirt road. Chea was a hero that day.

Later that night, Chea returned to the shack where Mr. Lee and Samang were stationed. He reported that the people at the county hospital couldn't do much for Veha other than give him antibiotics and a shot, so they ended up transferring him to the Siem Reap hospital. Not long ago, he was recovering from malaria. Now, Veha had to fight death again. The three returned to the village to inform Maly and Nhean. They stood and watched as Maly crumpled to the ground in tears while Nhean tried his best to keep it together for his sister. The only person who looked optimistic was Chea. In fact, he was smiling.

"He's going to be alive... I know it," he said.

THE VIETNAMESE INVASION

B Y THE END of 1978, there were rumors swirling around the village that Vietnam had invaded Democratic Kampuchea after months of small-scale border skirmishes. Whether or not the rumors were true, Mr. Lee felt a growing tension within the entire village regardless of rank. The work from the *chllop* team started becoming easier since the leaders in charge were more preoccupied with the movements of Vietnamese armies. Laxer supervision meant that people were not working as hard, and production slowed.

For Mr. Lee, the invasion gave him the strength and energy to climb again. Since joining the *chllop* team, he was expected to report to work at the break of dawn. He was always given the option to sleep in Brave Village after work, but he opted to stay at the jungle base because finishing work at sunset meant he was too tired to make the mile-long journey back. Being late to work generally wasn't tolerated, but the Vietnamese had made the *chllop* leaders oblivious to the lack of punctuality, so he began to make the trip more often. One day as Mr. Lee started walking back to Brave Village, he noticed that Khmer Rouge soldiers from other parts of the country had been entering and raiding the village at night to root out suspicious people that may be against the regime. All they did was ask if "so-and-so" lived there.

Mr. Lee had heard from Nhean and Maly that the regime was mainly targeting the "old people," the same people who provided the Khmer Rouge its backbone. The trust was gone, and the Khmer Rouge were purging each other from within. Panic and paranoia grew. When the raiders would return, some of the "old people" in the village started framing other villagers, mainly "new people," by lying about their identity, and telling the soldiers that another person was them. Mr. Lee lost many of his innocent friends because of it; they died for nothing. It was everyone for themselves, and no life was safe whether you supported the Khmer Rouge or not.

During recent town hall meetings, leaders had been urging anyone who was strong enough to hold a machine gun to join the army. However, they only wanted the enlistment of "old people" because the migrants from the city were still not trustworthy. Mr. Lee noticed this while working in the fields; the female leader would approach the young men and women while they were working and order them to fight the Vietnamese. She would look at people like Mr. Lee and Samang and tell them that they couldn't fight because they looked like "new people."

To Mr. Lee, it stung that he was still being discriminated against despite years of supporting the village's informal economy; to this day, Mr. Lee said it still "pissed him off." In the end, however, it turned out to be a blessing because Mr. Lee would never have to fight in the war.

For the villagers that did volunteer or were forced to fight, Mr. Lee learned that they were only trained to shoot a gun. In other words, there was no other formal combat training. During the town hall meetings, they would occasionally talk about what the Vietnamese would do to Cambodians if they were captured. For instance, the leaders once described a Vietnamese torture method called "Grandpa's Tea."

According to the leaders, the Vietnamese first prepared a big hole. When it was a sufficient size, they deposited captured Cambodians inside. In each hole, the Vietnamese would place three Cambodians in a triangular shape before burying them up to their heads with dirt. Their heads were used as a mount for a big pot filled with water. Then the Vietnamese would set a fire in the middle of the three heads so that they could boil their water to make tea.

As the Cambodians screamed and moved their heads in pain, the Vietnamese soldiers would sarcastically poke them with a stick to stop them from moving because then they would spill "grandpa's tea." As a result, the Cambodians were burned alive. In short, whether or not this story was a myth, it was used to brainwash the Cambodians to resist Vietnamese rule. It seemed to work because after the meeting, many people decided to enlist.

The last time Guang ever babysat Teen's daughter, Teen personally came and told her that he was ordered to transfer to Siem Reap to help fight against the Vietnamese invaders inching closer to the city. Teen brought her a basket of dried fish along with a collection of some of his tools. Before leaving, he told Guang that the other village leaders would take good care of her.

When Mr. Lee visited Guang after hearing the news of Teen's departure, she showed him the tools he left behind, which included some of the nicest he had seen in the village. One tool that caught Mr. Lee's attention was Teen's short axe, which he claimed. He also took some of Teen's sharp, shiny metal knives as well as his leather toolbelt. He figured these tools would help when he started climbing palm trees more regularly again.

Mr. Lee began wearing Teen's belt strapped with his tools around the village, and over the course of a few days, people began to recognize them from their previous owner. He was subject to a plethora of stares but it wasn't until a villager approached him that he understood why.

"Is that from Teen?" he asked.

"Yes," Mr. Lee said.

"This damn thing has killed many people. It may be possessed by a monster and could turn you into one if you are not careful."

Mr. Lee was baffled. He didn't reply because he feared that his words may come true. Then the villager started to slowly back away from Mr. Lee. Thankfully the demons from Teen's tools did not take over Mr. Lee's body, and he continued to use the tools even after his exodus from Preah Vihear.

Trigger Warning: Graphic Sexual Violence

The Vietnamese continued approaching to the point where the village leaders were too preoccupied to force anyone to work. Everyone was free of their obligations, so Mr. Lee moved back in with Maly and Nhean and started to regularly climb palm trees again. With more free time and an increased supply of *athuy*, the social circles under the palm trees returned. Not many village leaders came by, so most often it would only be the climbers. Outsiders who exchanged some food for a drink were also always welcome.

Recently, Khmer Rouge soldiers had been retreating from battles with the advancing Vietnamese Army, and some stumbled upon Brave Village as a refuge. During a routine gathering under the palm trees, two Khmer Rouge soldiers came to exchange some of their food for *athuy*. After the trade was complete, Mr. Lee invited them to join the rest of the group for conversation.

Both soldiers—Akra and Chan—looked to be around 25 years old. Akra had no problem integrating himself into the group and their conversations. He had a very outspoken and slightly boastful personality. Chann, however, was far more reserved, and was often silent, talking only if he wanted to contribute to whatever story Akra was telling. As the night dragged on, as everyone in the circle started telling stories about animal hunting, Akra started to feel the effects of *athuy* after finishing a few bamboo canisters.

"You all are not wild enough," Akra said before delving into a story. While he was still on the battlefield, Akra was part of a 40 to 50-man team that was assigned a female cook. When Akra and his team left to fight for the day, the cook would stay behind and was expected to have dinner ready for the entire team upon their return. One night, they came back to an empty table; the cook had failed to prepare any food. Akra, being one of the team's leaders, confronted the cook, whom he found resting in her hammock.

"Why isn't the food ready? Why didn't you go to work?" he asked.

"I was too sick. I could not move from my bed," she replied.

Akra, who had endured heavy losses of his troops from the Vietnamese that day, had little room for reasoning or patience. He snapped. Akra summoned two of his *chllop* soldiers to grab the cook and tie her to a nearby tree but not before he managed to strip her of her clothing. Then, her arms and legs were bound, spread apart on the tree trunk like a spider on a web.

Mr. Lee and the other climbers kept a blank expression as they listened to Akra's story. Mr. Lee was sure he knew where this story was headed, and he felt disturbed, but not surprised.

The cook was crying as she begged Akra not to kill her. "I still have my parents in the village who are very old, and my little brother is too young. I need to help take care of him."

"What? You don't want me to kill you?" Akra replied, almost sarcastically. "You want me to fuck you. Is that what you want?"

"Yes, you can do what you please with me. Just don't kill me."

Akra pulled out his knife. He glanced at his reflection on its bloody, dirt-stained metal, and then looked back at the cook. He walked close enough to be in stabbing range. "Well... I don't want to fuck you, but I will fuck you with this."

Akra shoved his knife up the cook's vagina. Then he twisted it at an angle so that he could continue his slice all the way up to her neck, cutting her open and exposing her organs. Mr. Lee and the other climbers looked around at each other, horrified. Still, nobody said anything.

The cook's organs started to spill out of her body cavity. She was apparently still alive because Akra could see her lungs move, and her heart, despite being exposed, was still beating. "Ok guys let's eat some virgin's liver for dinner," Akra said.

Akra pulled out her liver with his bare hands and took a bite from it raw. He passed it around to the two *chllop* soldiers still with him, and they took turns taking bites until her liver was gone.

Mr. Lee and I both sit and stare at each other in silence for a while. All I can hear is the sound of the pressure washer in the kitchen. Mrs. Lee is probably washing dishes. Finally, Mr. Lee continues. "Whether or not he was exaggerating, I believed him. I believed him because I knew how cruel those people were. They did things beyond your imagination."

Akra and Chann came to drink with Mr. Lee once a week. Akra would always bring his radio, and everyone in the circle would listen to the war updates from Phnom Penh. Mr. Lee knew enough Khmer by now to understand that the Vietnamese had entered through the eastern border and captured Phnom Penh. The Khmer Rouge were retreating into the jungles and Mr. Lee believed that liberation was near, that evil would finally be vanquished.

The Vietnamese troops were now closing in on Siem Reap. As more soldiers returned from battle to the village, they told Mr. Lee that the Khmer Rouge in Victory Village were dumping three to four dumpster truck's worth of people into a large, recently-dug hole. All the soldiers surrounded the hole with their AK-47's watching for any movement. No shot had been fired, but everyone was buried alive.

Prak, Mr. Lee's former instructor who had murdered Narith, had enlisted to fight for the Khmer Rouge as the situation in Siem Reap became more dire. It was late at night when Mr. Lee saw an army truck dropping off soldiers returning from battle at Angkor Wat to the town hall. Many villagers, including Mr. Lee, ran to see what was going on. Prak's father, a fairly dark-skinned man with streaks of gray hair, was among the crowd and he ran to a soldier who Mr. Lee assumed was a friend of Prak.

"Have you seen Prak?" his father asked.

Mr. Lee could tell from the soldier's face that the whole fighting force those past few weeks had been through hell. The soldier's hair was long and wild, he was emaciated, and his eyes begged for sleep. He stared at Prak's father blankly for a few seconds until finally he said, "We were fighting at Angkor Wat. The Vietnamese had us surrounded. The trucks came but there wasn't enough space in the back for everybody."

Prak's father had been squeezing the soldier's shoulders, clinging to every word. "Our commander asked if anyone wanted to fight to the death so that the others can survive, and

Prak was one of the ones who volunteered… He was already in the truck."

Prak's father let go of the soldier and shook his head. "Why does he have to fight so hard?" He turned around and tried to stifle his tears as he walked away. Samang had been right about Prak's fate, yet a father had still lost a son.

Mr. Lee was sitting outside one morning with Nhean while Maly, like most of the villagers, continued to sleep in the shack when the quiet stupor of the village was suddenly interrupted by a loud crashing of bamboo on metal. Off in the distance, he saw a small cluster of moving dots heading towards the direction of the village. As they got closer, Mr. Lee realized that they were Vietnamese soldiers in brown uniforms. They all had serious faces, their teeth blackened from eating jungle vegetables. Over the next few days, groups of 10-20 soldiers slowly trickled into the village. Throughout the village, whispers of "what are we going to do now?" spread like wildfire. Everyone felt panicked or tense, but Mr. Lee felt almost nonchalant. He had been desensitized. Everything he had heard and experienced up to that point made him expect the unexpected. The Vietnamese moving into the village was another day, another new chapter, and another new life to face.

As more brown uniformed Vietnamese soldiers trickled in, their overall serious mood faded, and the people in the village finally began to relax. To Mr. Lee, this was liberation. The soldiers started enforcing a curfew, but it wasn't very strict. For example, if someone were to be out at night past curfew, all the soldiers did was question that person and make sure they weren't an enemy. Most of the time the soldiers could tell the "new people" were not based on their physical features.

The brown-shirt soldiers also handed over the management of the village to the "new people." Most of the residents in Brave Village held no animosity towards the new leadership. All everyone wanted was a peaceful, civilized life. People around the village began to smile more; gone were the days where *Angka* forced everyone to wear straight faces. People from neighboring villages started to visit one another because the threat of being killed by guerilla soldiers hiding in the jungle was minimized. Everyone worked for themselves, not for the village, and a local economy of trading and bartering goods began to flourish.

The brown-uniformed soldiers were slowly replaced by an influx of Vietnamese soldiers in green uniforms who had started fighting under the Socialist Republic of Vietnam. They seemed much more relaxed compared to their brown-uniformed counterparts, which Mr. Lee later found out were a special team of seasoned fighters that led Vietnam in invasions.

Even though the new Vietnamese occupants knew no Khmer, they had translators who allowed them to communicate with everyone in the village. Mr. Lee was able to converse with some of them because they were of Chinese heritage. These new soldiers showed Mr. Lee pictures of their girlfriends and wives as well as the letters they sent. They told him how they yearned to see them again. Mr. Lee would ask the soldiers how long they had been away from their families, and rarely would he hear a response that was less than six months. The green-uniformed soldiers held a meeting and used their translators to ask if anyone in the village spoke Vietnamese. Surprisingly, two people Mr. Lee knew raised their hands and came forward. They probably hid their identity because the Khmer Rouge soldiers in Brave Village hated the Vietnamese. The next day Mr. Lee saw both of them in green Vietnamese army attire strapped with Ak47s on their backs with hand grenades all around their waists. Mr. Lee came up and asked them what happened after the meeting.

"I'm a translator for the Vietnamese army now," one of them said. They both smiled, relieved that they didn't have to hide anymore. Mr. Lee smiled too. "No, you guys are traitors, man!" He patted the soldier who spoke on the arm and laughed to make sure they knew that he was joking. "Just don't bully us around."

The newly appointed translators both laughed, and after a short conversation, they walked away.

During the Vietnamese occupation, Mr. Lee continued to climb palm trees so that he could sell palm sugar, palm juice and *athuy* to new visitors and current residents. If he was not trading under the palm trees, people would usually find him at Maly and Nhean's shack or with Guang in Perseverance Village. Since livestock, among other trades, had become privatized, Teng and Seng started raising and trading chickens under the bamboo poles that supported Guang's house.

Many newcomers to the villages were refugees escaping from conflicts in other parts of the country. Several of them visited Mr. Lee for *athuy* or Guang for chicken. Mr. Lee recognized one of the refugees amongst the flood of entering people. His name was Ang, and he used to go to school with Mr. Lee in Phnom Penh. Ang tried to escape to Thailand through the Damrei Mountains before their crossing quickly turned perilous, as landmines manifested the landscape, hidden beneath grass, trees, and other foliage. Every step felt like a game of Minesweeper, and for those who managed to survive, the Thai soldiers guarding the border turned them away.

It wasn't only the mountains; landmines littered the entire countryside. Ang recalled that he, alongside thousands of others, walked shoulder-to-shoulder on the main dirt roads which were sometimes as narrow as 18 inches wide. If someone tried to cut the line by stepping off the main road, there was a great likelihood the person would set off a landmine, needlessly killing at least 10-20 people. Ang saw human torsos, legs, and arms flying everywhere, sometimes landing on trees where they hung like some kind of grotesque ornament. For other people, the lack of food forced their bodies to shut down, and they died on the roads. There was a pond at one point in Ang's journey with muddy water that also had a reddish tinge from bodies and limbs that landed in it. For Ang and all the refugees, that pond was the only source of water they had, so there was no other choice but to drink from it. Mr. Lee heard many stories similar to Ang's as refugees kept flooding in.

Although Mr. Lee could've made plenty of money trading his goods for gold, he chose to give out a lot of his stock for free because one of Guang's lessons rang in his ears:

"My mom told me that I shouldn't rob a person of his gold when he is already in trouble," Mr. Lee says.

Refugees offered Mr. Lee payments of gold and jewelry for palm juice or *athuy*, but Mr. Lee saw the state some of them were in and refused. Teng and Seng were the same way with their chickens. Mr. Lee ran out of inventory rather quickly because he was always surrounded by hungry refugees, but it didn't bother him. In fact, it kept giving him a reason to climb. Mr. Lee felt blessed that he could share what he had and give back to people who weren't as fortunate. It felt justified when he would see the smiles on their faces after receiving free drinks or watch them bathe and play happily in the nearby stream as if they hadn't had clean water in ages. After all, he knew the hunger, fear, and exhaustion that these people had endured.

Among the refugees who trickled into the villages were some that were returning home. As Nhean and Mr. Lee was sitting in their shack watching the flow of refugees come through, Nhean suddenly stood up.

"Do you see that guy?" Nhean asked.

Mr. Lee looked over to where Nhean was motioning and saw a tall but lanky boy carrying heavy tools on his back. Then he started approaching the shack. It was Veha, and he never looked stronger and healthier.

Veha showed where the doctors had sewn his wounds from the boar attack. "There was a lot of fighting in Siem

Reap. They said it was the Vietnamese," he said. "Once they took over, people started leaving, so I took it as my chance to escape… I walked for days."

As Veha told the rest of his story, he was interrupted by Maly who had returned from the river and fell into her brother's arms, sobbing.

In Perseverance Village, Mr. Lee also witnessed what remained of Teen's family return: his wife, his three boys, and his "princess." Teen's wife looked empty. Guang spotted and called out to her.

"Boupha," Guang said. "Are you alright?"

Boupha ran up to Guang and sobbed into her neck.

"They killed him… they killed my husband."

One morning, Guang gave Teng some gold.

"Go to the Lao border and exchange this for some food," she said. Since the Lees had given most of their food away to refugees, they were in desperate need of sustenance. As restrictions on daily living were lifted, gatherings and parties became more frequent, and Mr. Lee found himself visiting his family more often to make up for lost time. Occasionally, he would invite his friends for a meal and drinks. It was always a tight fit with almost a dozen palm tree climbers including Davuth, and others like Maly, Nhean, and Samang all crammed into one tiny shack. Although there was a perception that all the "old people" were rotten and savage because they served the Khmer Rouge, Mr. Lee found that was not always the case.

"Some of them were as good as Jesus," he says. "Doesn't matter what their race, ethnicity, or organization is, there are good and bad people. Just because people think a certain group is bad, doesn't mean every individual in there is bad."

Guang was doing work outside her house when two Vietnamese soldiers walked past her, stopping to talk. Guang was very confused because she didn't understand a word of Vietnamese, so she requested for a translator. When the translator showed up, he asked the soldiers to repeat what they said.

"He wanted to say that watching you tend to the yard reminded him of his mother," the translator said.

"Oh, then make sure to tell him and his friend to visit for dinner if they are ever hungry!" Guang exclaimed.

When they heard the translation, they both nodded with big smiles. "They both say that you are so kind, everyone in the village is so kind." The soldiers kept talking. "They ask if it can be tomorrow evening?"

"Yes, tomorrow please come," Guang said.

As the soldiers left, the translator turned back around. "Can I come too?"

"Is there any way we could send mail to Vietnam?" Mr. Lee popped the question during the middle of dinner the next night. The room fell silent as the whole family stared at him. Mr. Lee had been wondering for weeks how he could communicate with Dak, his father, who may or may not still be in Vietnam. The translator asked the soldiers, and while Mr. Lee couldn't understand the conversation, he could tell that the soldiers seemed very excited.

The translator turned to Mr. Lee and said, "They said that it's their main job to deliver letters to and from this village."

Mr. Lee stood up. He still kept a slip of paper that had Dak's Saigon, or now Ho Chi Minh City, address written down.

"Do you think they can take some letters to our dad?" Mr. Lee asked.

"They said they could try," the translator said.

Since Teng had not returned from Laos, Seng, who had fully recovered from malnutrition in Siem Reap, wrote the first letter. They had no paper so he peeled off the label from a sardine can, which had littered the street since the Vietnamese arrived. He wrote a short message on the back of it.

We are still alive. If you get this letter, please write back.

When Teng returned, he brought with him a lot of canned food (mostly sardines), clothes, paper, and pens. Mr. Lee was overjoyed when he saw that he even brought instant noodles, something he had been craving for years. He thought that he wouldn't live to ever see them again.

After what seemed like a month of waiting, the two soldiers returned to Guang's house, bringing with them an envelope from Ho Chi Minh. It was from Dak.

Guang waited to open the envelope until the entire family was gathered. Once everyone recognized his handwriting, nobody could hold back their tears. Seng continued to write back and forth with Dak, using the paper and pens Teng had bought. He started explaining the family's situation in Democratic Kampuchea. Dak wrote back telling the family that they should return to Phnom Penh because it would be easier for him to send money and that it would be an easier way to get transportation to Vietnam. It had been settled then; Mr. Lee would be heading home, a home he hadn't seen for four years.

Guang triumphantly returned from Siem Reap holding papers in her hand which granted the Lee family permission to travel through all military checkpoints. They were signed and dated by persons of authority in Siem Reap and obtaining them was typically a slow process unless the people in charge were bribed with gold. Guang managed mostly without the bribes because she had connections, but giving away free chicken proved to be helpful as well.

"We leave the next day. Trucks are coming tomorrow for anyone with papers," she said.

When Mr. Lee boarded the back of the truck a day later, he looked down below and was greeted with the sight of everyone from the villages of Preah Vihear. They all stood by the dirt road, waving at the people departing. People Mr. Lee had been familiar with for years cried out at him to have a safe trip home.

"Come back and visit soon," a lot of them said.

Mr. Lee remembered when he was first forced to come to the village. How he vowed to never come back if he had the chance to leave. However, his departure was bittersweet. Mr. Lee was overcome with tears. He was leaving haunting memories of the Khmer Rouge behind, but he also left friends and a place he was forced to call home.

PART 3
EVIL'S EXODUS

LEAVING PHNOM PENH

I PEEK THROUGH THE screen door into the kitchen to see Mr. Lee sitting on a stool with one leg crossed over the other. He has glasses on, and his face is focused on a newspaper. My hands are holding a container filled with Filipino food I made for the Lees. Since the family always feeds me dinner while I'm at the restaurant conducting interviews, it has always been on my mind to return the favor. The food inside the container is chicken *adobo*, a classic Filipino staple dish of chicken coated in a soy sauce and vinegar sauce containing crushed garlic, ginger, peppercorns, and bay leaves.

I lightly kick the bottom of the door a few times since my hands are full, and Mr. Lee looks up from the newspaper. He lets me inside and points at the container.

"Whatcha got there?" he asks.

"It's Filipino food that I made for you guys."

Mr. Lee seems surprised. "No, you didn't have to do that," he replies. He almost sounds embarrassed. Now he knows how I feel every time they spoil me!

I keep insisting, and the Lees accept my gesture and agree to eat it for dinner. As Mr. Lee takes the container of adobo from me, I realize my hands are sticky from the sauce that dripped over. As I head to the sink to wash them, I turn to Mrs. Lee and say, "Make sure you eat this with rice." I then walk towards the front door into the restaurant, eager to hear about the journey out of Cambodia.

After a week-long journey, Mr. Lee could see the skyline of Phnom Penh from a distance. As the trucks entered the city, he saw that it was a shell of its former self. A lot of buildings were either damaged or in ruins by missiles, and many houses had been ransacked by looters, made evident by the torn down walls and floors which were popular hiding spots for storing gold. The country had been renamed again to the People's Republic of Kampuchea or the PRK, and the Vietnamese replaced Lon Nol's soldiers on the streets. All of a sudden, the trucks stopped at a curb.

"Everyone must leave. This is the final stop," the driver said.

Some people that disembarked started walking in various directions, probably to their former homes. Others laid out their mats and blankets ready to sleep right there by the curb.

An acquaintance in Perseverance Village had told the Lees that his family had already returned to Phnom Penh and reoccupied their old house. He offered them their place to stay for the night. Seeing as they really didn't have many other options, they all agreed.

The next morning, the acquaintance offered the Lees one of their properties as a temporary stay. Although a kind gesture, there was still an ulterior motive: to make the landlords and other returning residents believe the property was not abandoned. Mr. Lee and Seng spent the next few days reacclimating to the city, and when they returned to their old neighborhood, they found their apartment already occupied by another family.

Walking around the city felt strange. It had been many months since Phnom Penh was liberated from the Khmer Rouge, so the city had some time to return to normal before Mr. Lee arrived. However, daily city life now felt foreign after spending a large portion of his upbringing in rural Cambodia. Businesses were running, people were dining at restaurants, factories in the city were functioning, and traffic filled the streets.

A few days later, Guang returned home from the market distraught. Chang and Bieng rushed to relieve her of her groceries so she could sit down and collect herself. "Gia's dead," Guang said, as she continued to sob.

While she was at the market, Guang crossed paths with Gia's coworker, the same woman who left with Gia to the clinic before the infamous Cambodian New Year five years ago. Guang learned that nobody had been allowed to go home until the following morning. Once it came time to leave, it was too late. The Khmer Rouge had already invaded the city, and everyone at the clinic was trapped.

Gia, like everyone else, had relocated to the countryside. Her skills were well respected in the village she stayed in. She knew how to sew, fixing tears in people's T-shirts and knitting socks and hats for the village's babies. A lot of the "old people" asked her to live with them and be their daughter. Some even offered their sons for marriage.

She declined all of these gestures and chose to live with an aunt and her nephew who had both recently arrived in the village, despite warnings from others. In Phnom Penh, the aunt had owned a jewelry store and lived in a villa with maids and butlers. Everyone was supposed to be on equal footing in this new regime, but the village leaders were still conducting witch hunts against the rich, the educated, and the government workers. It was only a matter of time before her aunt would be discovered.

Eventually, the village leaders came to the shack in which Gia and her aunt were staying. The leaders led them away from the village, saying they were headed for Vietnam. Gia's co-worker heard from the villagers days later that everyone in the group was executed alive, and the babies and small children were grabbed by the ankles and had their heads slammed on rocks. That was Gia's fate.

Mr. Lee's eyes start to redden, and he has to pause.

"Every time I talk about her, it makes me want to tear up."

To have a favorable chance at starting a new life, Guang was told that she should find work with the new government because a job through them also came with housing. She was also told that the family could bribe their way for these jobs with about an ounce of gold. However, the Lees had no gold left.

In Preah Vihear, Dak mentioned in one of his letters to send some of the children to Ho Chi Minh City so that he could send them back with Vietnamese *dong* and some gold he had saved up. Dak didn't trust the postal service with sending large sums of money, and he was worried that they may move and switch addresses.

Teng and Chang were sent to see their father since they were the oldest out of the six, and were therefore independent enough to make the two-week long roundtrip. However, when they returned, they never brought the full amount with them because some of Dak's money was always confiscated due to "random" security checks at bus stations. Teng especially came home defeated whenever security took everything Dak gave him. There was even an instance where Teng was stripped of his clothes and given new ones to wear. Nevertheless, Guang eventually saved up enough gold to bribe the manager at a factory to hire her boys as government employees.

The manager would only accept two new workers, so Mr. Lee and Teng were given official employee IDs to commemorate their new job, while Seng replaced Teng in going to Ho Chi Minh City with his sister. The Lees also managed to secure a place to stay: a small, somewhat ramshackle apartment, but still an improvement from a bamboo shack in the jungle. Chang and Bieng also found odd jobs, while Guah stayed with Guang to help with housework. Over time, Mr. Lee adapted and felt comfortable in his new life. He was making money from the factory, and he spent a lot of his free time at the market nearby. It was simple, but life started to feel normal again. For Mr. Lee, there was no reason to leave.

After arriving home from work one day, Mr. Lee was confronted by his mother. She asked him to sit down with the rest of his siblings.

"We need to leave. We need to find real freedom. You are all still young, meaning that you all still have futures. You lost your childhoods and a chance at an education, but maybe… maybe we can go somewhere where you all can better yourselves," Guang said.

Guang saw the state their homeland was in, a country still ravaged by war, struggling to meet the needs of its millions of inhabitants. Stability and a bright future were questionable. Teng was excited by this announcement. He didn't recognize the city anymore, and he had been openly voicing his discontent. Chang, Bieng, and Guah also did not feel at home anymore, and Seng had always imagined a future similar to his father. Mr. Lee seemed to be the only one who felt differently.

"Why can't I just stay here by myself?" Mr. Lee asked.

Guang and his siblings responded to his request with silence and pointed stares. Guang then frowned and stood up to go outside. That night Mr. Lee heard his mother sobbing in bed. He started to think about what his father said before he left, about staying together. After everything the family endured, separating now would still not guarantee that they would later unite, and that was something he should value over his own content. Mr. Lee settled his internal dispute and told Guang the next morning that he supported her decision for everyone to leave Phnom Penh, maybe for good.

The plan was to leave for Thailand and claim refugee status, but leaving the PRK was considered treasonous. Not only that, but the Thai government had completely shut down their borders to refugees. At the same time, border smugglers between Thailand and the PRK were becoming more and more popular. Thai merchants used smugglers to enter the PRK, and likewise Cambodians in the PRK used smugglers to enter Thai refugee camps.

Once they reached Thailand, Uncle Qiang, one of Dak's brothers who immigrated to the United States after serving for the South Vietnamese Army, would try and sponsor the Lees to come live with him.

Teng had found a smuggler but was only able to bring one other person with him. He chose Chang. They would leave first, a week after Guang's proposition. No one was immune to tears that day because there was a real possibility they may never be reunited. Guang had also been in contact with another smuggler who finally agreed on a date to leave soon after Teng and Chang's departure. The smuggler, who introduced himself as Po, met Guang, Mr. Lee, Bieng, Guah, and Seng at the train station. With a glance, Mr. Lee knew he wasn't a native, which became more apparent as he spoke very broken Khmer. Mr. Lee's best guess was that Po was either Vietnamese or Chinese.

Po led the family outside the train station to a nearby parking lot where big commercial trucks were parked, and drivers outside were leaning on the side of their trucks smoking and conversing with one another. Po approached one of the truck drivers, talked to him briefly, and then handed him some Vietnamese *dong*. Po returned to Guang and the rest of the family to give them instructions.

"All of us will sit in the back of the truck," he said.

Po and the Lees shared the truck bed with multiple other passengers, nestled between crates, rice bags and other commercial cargo. It wasn't a military vehicle, but a truck with an elongated bed secured by a poled fence that added a few inches of protection for the cargo.

Mr. Lee doesn't remember much of the journey outside of constant checkpoints by Khmer or Vietnamese soldiers. Everyone was usually greeted with machine guns pointed at them followed by plenty of intimidating language. The soldiers often asked what business they had being in the back of the truck. Mr. Lee did all of the talking for his family, telling the soldiers that they were looking for separated family members believed to be close to the border in Thailand. Meanwhile, Po would sit in silence in the background. If Mr. Lee had told the truth and said that they were escaping to Thailand, there was a real chance that the family would be placed in a prison camp.

At some of these checkpoint searches, everyone was required to step outside of the truck, and on occasion, Mr. Lee would see the dead bodies of innocent people lined on the side of the road with gunshot wounds or missing limbs. Despite the Khmer Rouge being ousted from power, there were still conflicts caused by different armed factions within the country.

There were times when the ride became bumpy because the driver would take alternate routes away from the main road. He sometimes took sharp turns or sudden stops that would give even the strongest soul motion sickness. All of this was necessary to avoid the landmines that lurked beneath the foliage, waiting for the slightest pressure to detonate and destroy. Mr. Lee thought that the establishment of the PRK meant that travel would return to how it was before the Khmer Rouge took power, but he couldn't have been more wrong. In fact, it had only slightly improved.

The truck stopped at a town relatively close to the Thai border. The driver opened the gate on the truck bed and announced that this was as far as he could go. Mr. Lee disembarked with the rest of the passengers and stretched out his limbs. He started to wander and look around at all his new surroundings. It was a bustling town with concrete buildings and paved roads. It wasn't large enough to be considered the size of Phnom Penh, nor was it so rural that there were bamboo buildings. Mr. Lee had not wandered far from the truck, but as he walked back to where it was parked, it had already left. There was no sight of it, nor his family, nor Po. Now lost and with no other choice, Mr. Lee wandered the streets looking for any trace of his family when a man with semi-formal civilian clothing suddenly approached him.

"Hey brother, where are you going?" he asked, in a slightly aggressive tone.

"I'm just going to the store, and then back home," Mr. Lee said, in a perfect Khmer jungle accent. The stranger, who had acted suspicious towards him, immediately let his guard down. He probably thought Mr. Lee was Vietnamese due to his lighter coloring.

The stranger then told Mr. Lee to follow him, and since he didn't seem threatening anymore, Mr. Lee reluctantly agreed, eventually led to a small house. As the stranger opened the front door, there reeked a strong, sweaty, pungent smell. The inside of the room was equally horrifying.

There were Vietnamese people strapped to the walls. Some were tied upside down. One of them had a fish sauce bottle forced into his mouth. Everyone had been stripped naked, their bodies scarred and bleeding from being whipped, the blood congealing along cracks in the floor.

"This is what happens when I catch them," the stranger said.

In his head, Mr. Lee wanted to say that he had seen things worse than this. It wasn't right, but he had become desensitized to it. Mr. Lee made excuses not to stay long at the torture house, and then left for the streets again shortly after.

The sun was starting to set, and Mr. Lee still could not find any trace of his family, or Po, or anyone that was on the truck. His situation was looking increasingly dire; he had no money or place to stay, and was completely alone in a strange city. Why had they left the truck and disappeared without anyone thinking to tell him? Mr. Lee hadn't gone that far. The longer he walked, the more he felt like he was under a spell, his mind overwhelmed with people and an environment he didn't recognize, on top of the constant worry for his family.

Eventually, close to the center of town, he recognized two teenagers that were on the cargo truck with him: a brother and sister duo who both looked around 18-19 years old. The brother was holding a bucket, both of them probably heading for the river that was nearby, and as Mr. Lee approached the two, the brother called out to him.

"Hey, what are you doing here?" the boy said.

Mr. Lee explained to the two teenagers that he had been separated from his family, and that he needed to find them so that they could continue their journey to the Thai border. The teenagers' eyebrows furrowed, their faces lined with concern.

"Well for now, just come with us," the sister said.

The brother and sister duo introduced themselves as Krav and Vanna, respectively. Mr. Lee followed the siblings to the river where they all took a bath to freshen up.

"It's getting dark, you should stay with us tonight," Vanna said.

"Are you sure?" Mr. Lee asked.

"I'm sure. You can look for your family tomorrow."

As Mr. Lee followed the two home, Krav explained that they had family in Phnom Penh whom they went to visit, and the safest mode of transportation to and from the capital was to be smuggled. Mr. Lee arrived at their house, a small, concrete building, and was greeted by their mother, Phary. She beckoned the three of them inside and served Mr. Lee dinner. As they ate, Mr. Lee relayed the information he shared with Krav and Vanna to her.

"Son, are you sure you want to do this?" Phary asked. "From this point, it's really dangerous."

"What choice do I have?" Mr. Lee said. In his mind, no matter what, the family must stay together in the hopes of being reunited.

"I understand. Still, I insist that you stay in the city until you find your family," she said. "Also, there are many bandits that come out at night, and the soldiers won't help you either. Sleep here however long you need. It's safer."

Phary was a simple woman, as evident from her home. She hardly had any interior decoration like paintings or large furniture. Everything in her home served a purpose. It also seemed like Phary was connected with a smuggling ring similar to Po because outside under her porch awning were mats occupied with what Mr. Lee suspected to be refugees and/or other smugglers. Instead of having Mr. Lee sleeping outside with the rest of them, Krav and Vanna offered to share their bed with him.

Despite the hospitality and security, falling asleep that night was difficult. Mr. Lee could not stop thinking about his situation, about his family. From where he lay, he was facing a window, staring into the wilderness illuminated by moonlight. Except for the crickets chirping and the heavy breathing by Krav and Maly, it was peaceful. What if it was always this quiet? No landmines setting off, no gunshots, no screaming, no crying, no evil. However, reality returned in the form of a vehicle engine blaring through the quiet street.

The sound grew and the engine stopped. There was commotion through the wall behind him. The artificial flashlight beams joined the moonlight, bathing the house with light. Loud knocks threatened the bolts of the front door. Phary answered, and all Mr. Lee could hear were men asking a lot of questions. Mr. Lee couldn't decipher her response, but it was enough to make the interrogators leave. Mr. Lee closed his eyes again, and shortly after, he finally fell asleep.

The next morning, Phary explained that a few days ago, there had been plenty of bandits that came from the jungle to rob and kill the people in town. The soldiers from last night were patrolling to make sure no household was harboring any bandits. After eating a small portion of rice with half a dried fish for breakfast, Mr. Lee left to continue searching.

"If you can't find your family, remember that you still have this place," Phary said.

Mr. Lee walked down busy streets all morning, to no avail; he found not even a hint as to where his family might be. Phary had given him enough allowance to buy some street food, so he decided to stop by the local market for lunch. There he bought a small bowl of curry noodles and sat at the edge of the street so he could eat.

Suddenly Mr. Lee heard a heated exchange coming from a street food stall nearby. He turned his head towards the noise and saw a Vietnamese soldier trying to interrogate a young woman. She was next to a stall that sold dried fish, and she looked confused. All she could do was shake her head no and respond to him in Khmer. The soldier didn't seem angry. Maybe he mistook the young woman as Vietnamese because she, like Mr. Lee, also had fairer skin. Then as Mr. Lee looked more closely, he realized why soldiers were mistaking her for Vietnamese. The young woman was Bieng.

"She's Khmer! Why do you keep speaking Vietnamese to her!" the dried fish vendor said. The Vietnamese soldier eventually saw how hopeless the situation was and left. This was Mr. Lee's chance.

"We were looking everywhere for you!" Bieng cried, as she started hitting her brother. Her confused look from earlier morphed into one of relief. "We are staying with Po's uncle. It's about a 20-minute walk from here."

Bieng was at the market because she was buying food for dinner, enough for the whole family. Mr. Lee helped his sister finish shopping and followed her back to where the rest of the family was staying. Everyone relaxed after seeing Mr. Lee, although he could not escape a scolding from a teary-eyed, but irate Guang.

At this new house, Mr. Lee met Po's uncle, a short man with thinning gray hair. He looked as fair skinned as Po, which suggested he also wasn't ethnically Khmer. In the common room, the Lees were huddled around the old man as he explained to them the journey ahead.

"The path from here to Thailand is plenty more dangerous," he said. "You all risk being killed by bandits, soldiers, wild animals, and even other refugees... Honestly it's safer settling in this town. It is relatively peaceful here."

"There's nothing left for us here, but sadness," Guang said. Her tone suggested that she preferred dying than staying in the PRK any longer. Po's uncle turned to his nephew, who agreed to take them to another smuggler for the next step in the journey. Everyone was set to leave the next morning.

At the break of dawn, Po led the Lees to the edge of town where the entrance to the jungle was. They were met by a tall, muscular man whose demeanor reminded Mr. Lee of Teen and other killers in Preah Vihear. Mr. Lee's face must have indicated his concerns because Po quickly reassured him the man was not a bad guy. "He's one of my closest friends," Po said. The man was also a smuggler, except his main hustle was helping Thai merchants cross the border to sell goods in the PRK. However, this man had no truck or car with him, relying instead on a different mode of transportation.

"Bicycles?" Seng asked.

Po explained that to reach the refugee camps at the border, they had to enter discreetly. The camps only allowed specific personnel to enter and were heavily guarded. The path to enter one of the first camps was through the jungle behind them, and because it was too narrow to pass by car or truck, people had to either walk or bike through it to get to the camp by the border.

Guang used some of the remaining Vietnamese *dong* she had to purchase two bicycles from Po's friend. Mr. Lee would drive one bike with Guang seated behind him, Seng the second with Bieng at the back, and Po's friend would drive his bike accompanied by Guah. Although the bikes were designed for one person only, they had no other choice, squeezing together on the seat.

The path was more of a vague trail matted down by others who had already made the journey; there wasn't even a dirt road. The smuggler and Guah took the lead, with Seng and Bieng following behind them. Mr. Lee was at the rear, tailing both bikes, but the other two cyclists pedaled so fast that within a few minutes, Mr. Lee had completely lost them. Mr. Lee had to resort to following bike tracks left behind by previous cyclists. The weight of Guang, along with Mr. Lee's inexperience riding a bike, caused them to fall off multiple times.

Mr. Lee shakes his head and takes a sip of water from his cup. "I could just tell that her back was hurting. She was groaning from so much pain," he says.

While on the road, Mr. Lee witnessed the all too familiar scene of human suffering. Hopeful refugees were on the side of the road crying, some lying face-down on the dirt, probably on the verge of committing suicide. Others were more expressive with their despair, hitting their heads on rocks. Guang shook her head. She'd been desensitized as well, but sometimes she still had to look away.

Mr. Lee spotted a clearing in the jungle where many bikes were parked. There were street merchants selling food and water. However, to Mr. Lee's dismay, they only accepted Thai baht. Mr. Lee stopped the bike at the clearing so that the two could take a short break. After a few minutes sitting on the dirt, Mr. Lee and Guang were approached by a frantic-looking mother with her two little boys. She was a Chinese woman from Vietnam but spoke to them in Khmer.

"Are you both going to the camp? Do you know what the name of the camp is?" It was hard for her to speak because she couldn't stop crying. "My husband was caught by Pol Pot's men." Despite the Vietnamese ousting them from power, the Khmer Rouge, with help from Chinese funding, still maintained a presence in the PRK for another decade.

"Are you sure it was the Khmer Rouge? Or was it just another kind of soldier?" Mr. Lee asked.

"No, I'm sure. They were wearing black. They… they questioned my husband and he didn't speak Khmer, and before I knew it, they were pulling him into the jungle!" Mr. Lee looked around at her kids. One of them had blood flowing down the side of his leg. He later found out that he had jammed it on the bike wheel.

"Who are you waiting for?" Guang asked.

"My husband. Maybe he will still come out of the jungle. It's only been an hour."

Mr. Lee and Guang could not help the woman and left her there to wait for him. Everything was out of her control, yet she held onto the idea that maybe… maybe her husband managed to survive. It just wasn't realistic during those times,

Mr. Lee knew that. If the Khmer Rouge took you into the jungle, it was rare anyone ever saw you again.

Mr. Lee continued to follow the bike tracks until he reached another roadblock: a Khmer Rouge soldier watching from the side of the road with his rifle strapped around his back, his *krama* wrapped around his neck, wearing an all-black uniform. Mr. Lee stopped the bike and told Guang to walk the path. He would use himself as a diversion by biking towards the soldiers and engaging in conversation. Guang nodded, dismounted from the bike, and started walking. Mr. Lee biked to meet the soldier with no plan on what to say. He looked around and saw that there was a middle-aged Khmer woman next to the soldier selling bottled water. When Mr. Lee saw her, he knew what he was going to do. The soldier examined him, observing Mr. Lee from head to toe, then looking at his bicycle and then back to him.

"Where are you coming from?" he asked.

"Preah Vihear. I'm looking for my sister. I also want to buy some water," Mr. Lee said.

The soldier must have noticed the thick rural accent Mr. Lee had developed because he didn't ask any further questions. In fact, his demeanor relaxed, and he even cracked a smile.

"Well considering you are one of us, I think the water should be free," he said. The soldier looked at the woman next to him and she nodded. She handed Mr. Lee a cup of water. The soldier saw Guang and tried to interrogate her as well, but Mr. Lee told the soldier that she was his mother. After that he didn't seem to care anymore. Mr. Lee had a pack of cigarettes in his pocket and offered some to the soldier. He happily took one, and they both stood there smoking.

A pair of women that looked to be in their mid-20s walked by. The soldier stopped and beckoned them towards him. They both looked at each other, confused, and walked over. He asked them the same question he asked Mr. Lee.

"Where are you guys going?"

Again, the two women looked at each other. They didn't answer. Both still had looks of bewilderment upon their faces. Mr. Lee started to worry for them.

"Do you speak Khmer?" the soldier then asked.

There was still no answer, and Mr. Lee really started to worry now. The two women couldn't understand Khmer. Then Mr. Lee took a chance and spoke to the women in Mandarin.

"Chinese?"

Immediately they said yes.

"Are you guys trying to go to the camp?"

They said yes again.

"Ok, I will deal with him. Don't say anything."

Mr. Lee turned to his new Khmer Rouge friend and told him to let them go.

"These two girls seem very sick because they aren't making any sense. I think they are crazy," he said.

The guard started laughing.

"Ok, then leave!" he said, trying to wave off the two Chinese women.

"Go, go and leave," Mr. Lee said in Mandarin.

As Mr. Lee watched the women walk further away, he looked ahead in that same direction for Guang, and saw that she was almost out of sight.

"I also have to leave now," Mr. Lee told the soldier.

"It was good talking to you," the soldier said.

Mr. Lee mounted his bicycle once again and started pedaling. First, he caught up with the Chinese women and stopped to ask about their situation. They told him that their smuggler abandoned them when he saw the Khmer Rouge soldier. After all, smugglers were automatically killed if they were caught taking people out of the country. Mr. Lee couldn't offer them a ride on the bike, so he wished them good luck and pedaled up to Guang.

They eventually reached a barbed wire fence, and unfortunately, it was guarded by Khmer soldiers dressed in green camouflage. They were a part of the Khmer People's

National Liberation Front or the KPNLF, one of the main military resistance groups that formed and fought against the Khmer Rouge regime. They were in control of this refugee camp. Just like all the village leaders from Preah Vihear, they were vast and muscular. Some were shirtless, and they all had long hair. They were sitting on the ground playing cards, smoking cigarettes, and drinking. Since they were blocking the way into the fence, the original plan of sneaking inside wasn't an option. Mr. Lee had no choice but to disturb them.

"I want to go inside the camp to look for my sister. We have been separated for years… My mom is also old and sick, and she wants to see her daughter one more time."

"Are you Vietnamese or Chinese?" one of the soldiers asked. He had hair so long that it brushed against his bottom.

"Chinese," Mr. Lee replied.

"Ok go in."

Mr. Lee couldn't believe it. He wondered what would've happened if he had answered Vietnamese (probably not a good outcome from his experience). There had been growing anti-Vietnamese sentiment among Khmers even before Vietnamese occupancy. The long-haired soldier stood up and pulled the upper half of the barbed wire with his bare hands, providing Mr. Lee and Guang an opening through the middle of the fence.

The camp itself didn't look any better than Preah Vihear. Most of the shelters were the same bamboo and straw shacks in the shantytown Mr. Lee used to live in. Some refugees were a little better off with tents. The field surrounding the shacks had no life, no grass, just dirt. The camp didn't look like an established village or town; it was clearly run down and haphazardly made to accommodate the influx of refugees. Seng, Bieng, and Guah had arrived first and were waiting at the intersection of a busy main road. After a tearful reunion, a Khmer man who looked to be in his fifties approached and greeted the five of them.

"Are you both new here?" he asked.

Mr. Lee told him what he had been saying to everyone: they were trying to find his sister.

"Don't worry, you both are safe here."

The man led the family to his office, a bamboo hut. Inside was a bed where Guang, Bieng, and Guah would sleep, and there were two benches outside for Mr. Lee and Seng. The next morning, the old man returned and noticed Guang still struggling in pain from the falls she sustained during the bike ride. He escorted the family to a large, spacious white tent with a red cross above the entrance. Inside were rows of cots three feet apart, one of which was for Guang. He then turned to her four children and explained that the cots were only for the sick but finding an area to sleep inside the tent was allowed. He also said they would be fed twice a day starting with a meal in a few hours.

When the meal finally arrived, it was the best Mr. Lee had eaten in over a week. It was a Chinese stir fry of beef and broccoli served on top of a bed of warm white rice. The meal even came with a hot soup.

Despite a warm welcome, their journey wasn't over. When the kind old man returned to check on the family, Mr. Lee asked him if they were at Khao-I-Dang. The answer was disappointing. They weren't even in Thailand; they were at the KPNLF-controlled Nong Samet refugee camp, also known as "007," which bordered Thailand. Seeing the dismay on everyone's faces, he again reassured the family that the camp was safe and then left again.

That night, a mysterious curly-haired man entered the tent and started talking one-on-one with all the families inside. Eventually, he reached Guang's cot with all four children present and explained that he was smuggling people across the border into Thailand. His plan was to leave as soon as he could find two more refugees to come with him. Mr. Lee expressed his interest to go to Khao-I-Dang so that he could reunite with his other two siblings already there.

"We have a deal with Thai soldiers. They will let us into that camp, but we have to leave now because it is getting really dark," the curly-haired man said.

He gave the family a little time to think it over, and if two of them decided, he would be waiting not too far from the tent. Again Mr. Lee, in disagreement with the rest of his family, expressed interest in leaving. Either they did not want to risk it or they were still too tired from the last journey to move. Guang reluctantly, though disapprovingly, said Mr. Lee could leave if he wanted to. Although he didn't want to separate from his family again, leaving with the curly-haired smuggler could help build a connection for the rest of his family to sneak into Khao-I-Dang in the future.

Mr. Lee rushed out of the Red Cross tent trying to locate the smuggler. He asked the people close by if they had seen a curly-haired male nearby. A man pointed him to the direction of the smuggler's house; however, the house was empty when Mr. Lee went to check. The person in the neighboring house said the smuggler left about 15 minutes prior with a family, and then pointed to the jungle behind him. Given the information, Mr. Lee sprinted into the pitch-black jungle to catch up with him. Mr. Lee's voice echoed as he called out for his ticket to Thailand. His bare feet sloshed in mud as rain started pouring. Several minutes passed with no answer until finally, he was too tired to continue. Defeated, Mr. Lee headed home, drenched and muddy.

Guang wore a surprised look as she saw her son emerge from the tent entrance. Mr. Lee explained that he was too late and went straight to where his siblings were and collapsed, exhausted from the toil of the past few days. Not long after, he was awoken by the beams of flashlights through the tent flaps. He started to hear whispers and laughter from the people wielding them, probably soldiers. The screams came not long afterwards, followed by harsh commands. Some were distant, others were closer to the tent. It repeated sporadically, making it impossible to fall asleep. Mr. Lee started to notice a pattern. All the screams came from women.

The next morning, Mr. Lee walked around the camp and approached a group of refugees. He asked if they heard screams last night. One of them responded.

"Every night, the soldiers will just pull out women, sometimes even teenagers… whomever they want… and gang rape them," he said

Mr. Lee thought about Bieng and Guah and wondered if they were going to be safe.

"A lot of women try to make themselves look really ugly. They use scissors to cut their hair short to look like men, and some will smear dirt on their faces. Sometimes it doesn't help though," the man continued.

Another refugee in the group was sitting on the ground, and he looked up at Mr. Lee.

"My wife was pregnant, still pregnant... the soldiers knew that. One night they tried taking her, but I begged them not to, and even offered to cut some wood or do something for them so that they would leave her alone. They said that they would leave her alone and left... The next night they came back anyway, and this time they took her away."

The man looked down to the ground again. It was a chilling reality at the camp. Thankfully, the KPNLF soldiers never entered the Red Cross tent, but the screams never stopped.

Everyday volunteers from the Red Cross would visit the tent. Guang was still in severe pain from her back, and she could barely move to get out of bed. Eventually, Bieng couldn't bear to watch her mother in so much pain anymore and walked up to one of the volunteers. She approached a dark-haired woman who was from France.

"Can you help my mom?" Bieng asked in French.

The volunteer walked back with Bieng and used her as a translator to talk to Guang. After Guang explained her back pain to the volunteer, the French woman left and came back with two Khmer volunteers carrying a stretcher. They moved Guang to another white tent nearby where she was given medicine, and hot food was provided to the rest of the family. They were invited to stay overnight. The next day, the same French woman returned to check on Guang. When she asked for any updates, Bieng made another request.

"We need to get out of here as soon as possible because our brother and sister are at a camp in Thailand called Khao-I-Dang. We don't want our family to stay separated," Bieng said.

The volunteer's face hardened. She warned about the dangers of entering Thailand, and the risk she faced smuggling people over the border. Despite that, she offered to take the family, not to Khao-I-Dang, but to another border camp outside Thailand. She said that they could be placed on a waiting list to cross the border into Chonburi, which would allow them passage into the United States. The Frenchwoman led the five of them to her white Toyota and instructed them to lie down on the bed of the truck. Then she loaded cargo in-between and around everyone, and finally covered the truck bed with a long tarp.

By a stroke of luck, Thailand seemed feasible. Soon Mr. Lee would be leaving the only country he ever knew. A place where he grew up, but also a place that caused so much sadness and pain. Mr. Lee was closer to leaving home for good.

The French woman dropped them off at a small Red Cross tent where the officials inside registered everyone's name and age, as well as the number of people in the family, and the number of dead or separated family members. This new camp, called the NW9, was established for Vietnamese refugees. It looked no different from 007; the bamboo pole and hay roof shacks and tents lined the dirt streets for miles, and everyone slept either on tarp mats, or directly on the ground. The camp was still controlled by KPNLF soldiers, but since Mr. Lee was so close to the border, he sometimes dealt with Thai soldiers.

After the registration process was completed, the Lees were led to a 10x10 dirt plot already erected with a bamboo shack. They were also given a blue tarp mat so that nobody had to sleep on the ground. During the first week, Guang suffered the most. Her back was still in plenty of pain, and it became almost impossible for her to sleep because of the ground's hard surface. In an attempt to ease their mother's agony, Seng and Mr. Lee chopped a few bamboo trees into smaller poles which they stacked to make a bed for Guang. Mr. Lee still carried his hammock and tied it on opposite poles of the shack while the rest slept on the tarp.

Day-to-day life at NW9 was dull at best, or as Mr. Lee describes it, "same shit, different day." He would wake up when the sun rose to do his business and then wait for his first meal. They ate two meals a day, mostly canned sardines. Other times it was vegetable soup over rice. And occasionally, they received instant ramen noodles. There were Thai merchants everywhere selling various goods at the camp; however it was all very expensive. The merchants only accepted Thai *baht*, and if a refugee wanted to trade gold for cash, the merchants would give outrageous exchange rates. Therefore, buying things like sugar or cigarettes was unrealistic. Mr. Lee couldn't even afford to buy a shirt from the merchants to cover up his bare chest.

"It was sickening. It's greediness. A pack of cigarettes was probably $10, which is a lot for refugees to afford. I mean who got the money for that at a refugee camp, man?"

Since cigarettes were so expensive, whenever there was a click of a lighter or the smell of tobacco in the air, it attracted a swarm of smokers. Mr. Lee was guilty of this as well as he developed a habit in Preah Vihear. The rainy seasons would have been unbearable if he wasn't a smoker because gnats would swarm over his ears and face. Smoking was like bug spray in Preah Vihear because it kept the bugs at bay. Tobacco was grown in the village, so most people carried sandwich bags full of it. When people wanted to smoke, they would roll the tobacco in leaves. It wasn't just Mr. Lee though, his entire family smoked to keep the insects away.

Mr. Lee still had a pack of cigarettes he had been saving from Phnom Penh, and when he lit one, at least 20 smokers approached him asking for a hit. Mr. Lee was not going to deny them relief, so he passed the cigarette around. Once it reached him again, there was almost nothing left.

The family was supposed to receive ten gallons of water a day, but most of the time it was only five. The water was used for everything: cooking, bathing, cleaning, and drinking. Other days they only received a bucket. Sometimes Mr. Lee would trade a cigarette for water, and he also helped Seng dig deep ditches close to their shack so they could catch rainwater. He and Seng had to stay diligent and make sure strangers didn't find it.

Further into Thai territory, about 200 yards from the camp, was a 15 foot ditch. At the bottom of the ditch were many other man-made holes, also for catching rainwater. If it rained overnight, Mr. Lee would hear buckets clanking at 3:00 a.m. and by the time the sun rose, all the rainwater would be gone. Mr. Lee would see people using spoons to scoop up the remnants. Over the ditch was a patrol of Thai soldiers guarding the border, fingers poised on the trigger, ready to shoot at any time.

Trying to climb over the ditch resulted in the Thai soldiers putting the offender in the "monkey house," a small cage too low for someone to stand up, and too narrow for someone to sit down. The offenders were usually left in the "monkey house" overnight, and once released, the offenders started walking like a monkey because their bodies were stuck in a squat position for so long.

There were occasional skirmishes between Thai and Cambodian soldiers resulting in many being shot by stray bullets. As Mr. Lee describes it,

"We were like fish in a shark tank."

A nice improvement from the 007 camp was the ability to contact the outside world like the United States and Australia. There was an area at the camp where people could go to receive mail, and refugees would volunteer to sort it. Uncle Qiang had been sending money after hearing from Dak that Guang and four of her children made it to NW9. Dak also continued to send money, as well as his brother Heng in Macau. Mr. Lee believed, however, that the five of them only received 50% of the money sent because at the post station, volunteer refugees were often caught stealing mail and packages. Mr. Lee would see volunteers place envelopes in the light of the sun to see if there was a shadow that looked like money. Other angry refugees would see this and proceed to start fights. One time, Guang handed Mr. Lee a slip of paper to pick up a package from Heng, and when he went to the mailing station, the people at the desk said that somebody had already claimed the package.

Refugees from the Cambodian camps like 007 would arrive via military trucks twice a week. A lot of them were women, and some looked badly bruised and beaten. Mr. Lee recalled seeing a young woman from 007 with holes in her palms, and he learned that the KPNLF soldiers had nailed her hands on a board to restrain her because she resisted being raped by them.

The only aspect of NW9 that really brought any life into such a dull and depressing place was music. The Vietnamese refugees would often congregate with buckets they used to beat like drums, and other refugees would start singing. Mr. Lee couldn't understand anything, but he enjoyed seeing some joy and community. However, even that was often thwarted by Thai soldiers who would tell them off for being loud and fire warning shots in the air.

At the NW9 there was a wooden notice board that was updated every morning with a typed list of refugees being transferred to Chonburi. After about 6 months of waiting, Mr. Lee finally saw his name along with Seng, Bieng, Guah, and Guang. They boarded a bus, and within a couple of hours, arrived at the Chonburi Transit Center, met by the smiling faces of Teng and Chang fully dressed in civilian clothes. They were both notified by the United Nations High Commissioner for Refugees (UNHCR) that their family members were arriving. A cameraman was with them to take a family photo.

Teng and Chang took the family to a restaurant to celebrate. The server came and asked everyone what they wanted to drink. Out of nostalgia, Mr. Lee asked for a Coca-Cola since it had been over 5 years since he tasted one. Teng leaned over to Mr. Lee and suggested he drink something else.

"They have something better than that. Sprite!" Teng said.

Mr. Lee had never heard of that drink before, but he trusted his older brother, and told the waiter to change his drink to this Sprite. To this day, it's still Mr. Lee's favorite soda. The restaurant also had a T.V. mounted on the wall playing a Hong Kong action movie. Mr. Lee asked himself if he was dreaming. All of this felt too good to be real.

Chonburi was luxurious compared to the other two camps. Instead of bamboo shacks, it felt like a small urban city. The streets were lined with white concrete buildings, some containing restaurants and small businesses. The unit Mr. Lee stayed at was separate from Teng and Chang who had arrived at Chonburi before them from Khao-I-Dang, and it included luxuries like mats and blankets, things Mr. Lee hadn't had in months.

There didn't seem to be a problem with refugees stealing mail in Chonburi because Mr. Lee started seeing an increased amount of cash in every letter. He bought himself a pair of jeans, more shorts, a pair of tennis shoes, and several t-shirts. Dak also sent him a watch that he started wearing every day.

Uncle Qiang had been in contact with the Lees and the UNHCR since he was their sponsor to the United States. The Chonburi Transit Center was the most important stop because this was where the Lees finalized their immigration paperwork. Uncle Qiang had already been in communication with Teng and Chang. It was then that Mr. Lee learned that Teng had become a translator for Chinese and Khmer speaking refugees for the UNHCR. The Chonburi camp was not meant for extended stays; once refugees finished their immigration paperwork, they would immediately be sent to their next destination. In the short time before leaving for the

United States, Teng helped Seng obtain a role as translator as well for his area while Chang spent plenty of time with Guang and her sisters. The two would often treat the family to dinner.

Teng and Chang were the first to leave because they had arrived at Chonburi first. Once they left, Seng and Bieng spent most of their free time voluntarily tutoring other refugees in English. They had managed to obtain a book detailing the essentials of the English language, and Mr. Lee would sit in lessons sometimes; however, most of the free time he did have, he spent exploring. There were several street-side photographers everywhere he went. The photographers offered photos in exchange for money. To their delight, Mr. Lee always asked for one. When Mr. Lee wasn't posing for photos, he was enjoying a can of Sprite or chatting with the other refugees over some street food.

A couple weeks after Teng and Chang's departure, the remaining five members of the Lee family were called from the intercom to report to the immigration office. Once there, they were met with a Thai worker from the UNHCR. Since nobody had any official documentation like birth certificates, the immigration office had to legally give everyone a new identity. The woman at the desk asked each person to verify their age, birthplace, and other personal information. However, if it seemed like they were lying, the woman questioned them.

"You look so young!" the woman exclaimed to Mr. Lee. "You can't be that old." She ended up lowering his actual age by three years. Since he couldn't remember his actual birthday, he was given a new one. Mr. Lee didn't care at the time, but after being in the United States for a while, he realized that she was the reason he was late on his retirement pension.

Due to several years of malnutrition, everyone naturally looked smaller and younger, so they all had their ages lowered. Bieng was lowered seven years, and Seng, who was lowered five years, suddenly became Mr. Lee's younger brother. Whenever the interview was over, Guang was given a cloth bag and a lecture explaining how important its contents were; losing the bag meant losing your identity. Within the next few days, the Lees were interviewed by representatives from the U.S. and after a week-long process, they were finally approved to immigrate to the United States.

We wrap up for the day after five hours, the longest interview by far. Mr. Lee has unbelievable stamina when it comes to talking. He even asked multiple times if I could still continue because he noticed moments when my attention waned.

I walk in the kitchen and see that my glass container has been cleaned and is now drying on the dish rack. Amanda is sitting on a wooden stool on her phone while her mother is still working and looks up from her phone when she hears me enter.

"Dude that chicken stuff you made was so goood!" Amanda says.

"I only had one piece; Amanda ate most of it," Mrs. Lee says. "I also really liked it."

Next to Mrs. Lee is a small bowl which holds a chunk of chicken on top of a bed of rice coated in *adobo* sauce. The last piece is for Mr. Lee.

PHILIPPINES

My parents recently returned from a trip to the Philippines, and as usual they came back with a suitcase full of packaged foods not found where we live in Little Rock, AR. One of my aunts sent a couple of plastic containers filled with *adobong mani*, which are deep fried salted peanuts with garlic. For an added kick, she added some small red peppers in the mixture and tiny pieces of dried fish for extra flavor. My parents gave me one of the containers to take back with me to Conway.

After nearly four months, my last interview with Mr. Lee soon approaches. He had prefaced that his last stop before reaching California was the Philippines. He had talked about the clear blue water on the beaches, and the remoteness of the nature around him. He also mentioned its diverse and delicious food, the happy-go-lucky locals, and the laid-back island vibes. He equates the Philippines to paradise, all of which I am fondly familiar with. I miss the Philippines for the same reasons, especially since I only visit family there about every two years.

To celebrate the end, it dawned on me that since this last interview will be about his time in the Philippines, I should again offer a gift of cultural exchange. Instead of making chicken *adobo* again, why not share some premade *mani*?

As I walk through the screen door, Mrs. Lee is cutting and prepping chicken breast as usual; Mr. Lee is doing work with some other kitchen equipment. It's December, and the air has gotten colder. Mr. Lee has switched out his t-shirt with a longer sleeved one, although the shorts and Nike slides remain. He greets me and pours a styrofoam cup of water from the tap as usual. As we talk in the kitchen, I notice that his voice sounds hoarse.

"I've been dealing with a scratchy throat," he says. "I apologize in advance if it affects the audio recording."

"Don't worry about that. It'll be fine," I say.

We take our usual seats, mine in the booth, his in the gray metal chair. Then, I grab my backpack and take out my container of *mani*. Since I also had time to run to the oriental store, I picked out a drink that I think he would enjoy. Mr. Lee points to the peanuts and the small carton of *calamansi* juice.

"What you got there?" he asks.

I first tell him about the salted peanuts and then about the *calamansi* juice. I explain that *calamansi* is Philippine lime, and that one of my favorite drinks before immigrating to the United States was—and still is—*calamansi* juice. I thought of Mr. Lee when I bought the juice because of his stories selling *athuy* in Preah Vihear. Minus the alcohol content, whenever he talked about the combination of a sour and sweet drink, it reminded me dearly of *calamansi* juice. Tonight, I want to at least attempt to emulate a night under the palm trees.

"This may taste really similar to *athuy*. Try some and tell me if it does," I tell him.

I open the carton and pour some juice into the bottom end of the cap. I hand it to Mr. Lee, and he points the cap towards his mouth, letting the short flow of yellow lime juice stream out.

"Wow this is really sweet!" Mr. Lee nods his head in approval. "It's similar but it's not that sour. Thank you though because this juice will help with my throat." His cheeks plump as a smile cracks his face. He immediately stands up and walks into the kitchen to grab another styrofoam cup so that he can pour himself some more juice. I take a sample from the cap myself and then I wince because the poor guy isn't even trying good *calamansi* juice. Of course, nothing will ever beat the freshly made version in the Philippines, but it was the best I can do.

As Mr. Lee pours some *calamansi* juice for himself, I dump some *adobong mani* into the bottom of its cap to use as a little bowl. We sit and talk for awhile, chewing on peanuts and drinking lime juice, about our lives and about the book before diving straight into the interview. It was out of courtesy at first but has become a tradition over time. The conversation takes an interesting turn when Mr. Lee asks me a question:

"Do you know what you are going to name the book?"

I had started exploring that very question the closer I reached the end of Mr. Lee's story. Some person in my life, maybe a teacher or one of my bookworm friends, or maybe a source I found on Google, told me that a good title can come from a notable piece of text or quote that defines the piece as a whole. I looked through my written audio transcriptions and noticed a phrase that ignited a lightbulb in my head.

"Thank the Evil."

Mr. Lee looks at me a little confused, so I clarify.

"It's something you said in an interview."

Mr. Lee crosses his arms, his facial expression doesn't change, still a little confused. He leans back in his seat as if trying to process what I have said, before responding with, "I like it."

"Do you think you can tell me what you meant by thanking the evil?"

Mr. Lee uncrosses his arms and with his left hand, he starts rubbing his thighs, trying to think about what to say next. His gaze goes to the ceiling again, and after a few seconds, he looks back at me and responds.

"Well… It sounds contradictory. In my mind, appreciate what you have. Don't feel bad for what you don't have. Those people in Cambodia were so evil, but my thanks to them wasn't that they killed people. My thanks to them was blessing me for letting me live. I had to thank them for sparing my life… I'm thankful for my life. My life in Preah Vihear was a lot better than a lot of people's even though it was still pretty terrible. However, I feel like you shouldn't compare your life because then you will never be satisfied. If you have one-million dollars in the bank and you compare it to someone who has one billion, how will you ever be happy? When I compare my life now in America to the life I used to live where there was no food or a proper house, I feel so blessed."

"I had to cherish the good when all the bad things were happening around me. I'm supposed to want to kill or get revenge on the Khmer Rouge for taking away my childhood, that I should never forgive them, but that's not right… It's not good to keep that anger or hatred inside your mind. It's not healthy… I mean, you don't want to carry those feelings into your heart and live like that for the rest of your life."

"I want to thank the evil because they spared my life. I'm still alive. Whatever already happened I can't save it back. I lost Gia; she's not gonna come back. I still have brothers and sisters around, can't say the same for some people I know. I can't be sad about it for the rest of my life. It's not the point of continuing to live. I understand that there are a lot of obstacles in life, but I still try and appreciate what I have in that moment. I think I am so happy right now because I knew what it was like to lose it, and I fought to get my happiness back."

"From my childhood, I learned that you can't be rich with just material goods. You have to live rich inside your heart. You have to cherish things in life. A lot of people I know have all this material stuff, but they are not happy. Some of them got very sick… money cannot buy your health sometimes. As long as you enjoy what you are doing, it doesn't matter how much money you make. I'm just so happy that I got all the food I want, and I have my house… my restaurant too."

"I think a lot of us are starting to realize that. A lot of parents want their kids to be doctors or lawyers or CEOs, which is good for them. But what's the point of forcing someone into something that they don't like? I was forced to live in the jungle, so I know how that feels. I've been forced to do things I didn't want to do, and it made life feel so unmeaningful. It made no sense… it was senseless! I told Amanda: whatever you do, just do something you want to do. I can't force her to be a doctor, hell man I don't want to be one either."

"For a while all I asked for was enough food. I never thought of making one thousand or one million dollars. Now when I see people who already have their needs met always wanting more stuff, I just wonder, "What more do you want?"

Mr. Lee and his family had a quick two-day layover in Manila before they would be transferred to a new camp. They stayed in a suburban one-room apartment in Metro Manila. Since there was no curfew or walls separating refugees from the rest of society, and with nothing to do but wait for meals, Mr. Lee decided to explore the city by himself. The street he lived on was quiet. There weren't many people walking around, and there wasn't much on the street outside of residential buildings. As he walked about the block, he reached a major intersection that morphed into an even larger street. Mr. Lee described the chaos.

"Man, there was a big street, and people, and traffic. You hear all those noises, and it was so crowded!"

It reminded Mr. Lee of how Phnom Penh used to be, although he never remembered it to be as chaotic. Watching the life of the city brought tears to his eyes. He walked down that street and started looking inside stores. He saw street food stands and bought himself a snack. Losing track of time, he walked around for what could have been hours before eventually returning to the apartment for dinner.

When the UNHCR was ready, a bus was prepared to relocate the refugees to their new temporary home. The journey took about a day with three stopovers, all requiring them to transfer buses. The roads were rough as they navigated through underdeveloped and windy mountain paths, but otherwise the trip was uneventful.

The refugees arrived late at night at Barangay Sabang, Morong Bataan. The refugee camp was a large facility within the province that probably took 40 minutes to walk from end-to-end. The camp was known as the Philippine Refugee Processing Center, and it was used as the final stop for many Indochinese refugees before being resettled to another nation, primarily the United States. The people who worked at the camp assigned all the new refugees to temporary housing, which like Chonburi, were real buildings and not wall-less, bamboo shacks. White concrete made up the exterior, floors were wooded inside, and the roof wasn't made of hay or straw. These buildings even had built-in electricity. Mr. Lee and his family were assigned a billet in Neighborhood Eight, its location close to many outdoor markets. These markets were also where most motorelas—a motorized tricycle with an attached cab—would be, waiting to provide public transportation for locals and refugees alike. The camp was relatively close to the beach, and almost every day Mr. Lee, who was now 20 years old, and his new friends from the refugee camp would take a motorela for two *pesos* from the market to the beach where they could swim in the sea and lounge in the sand. Like in Manila, there was no curfew, and there were no guards bullying anyone around. In fact, Mr. Lee didn't really recall even seeing many police officers. At night, he would head back to the market to buy street food and a few beers. It felt like true freedom, like paradise. Life had never been so perfect for Mr. Lee, and at times he even forgot that at any moment he could be leaving for the United States.

Before he could leave though, he had to take classes to help himself and other refugees assimilate and transition to life in the United States. Mr. Lee had to learn how to interview for a job, how to open a bank account, how to go grocery shopping, and how to pump gas. Of course, they also learned how to speak English.

"Not trying to brag, but I was the best in my class," Mr. Lee claims.

Every time a class graduated, the entire school was invited to throw a party for them. There would always be plenty of food, sodas, music, and dancing.

Some refugees started small businesses selling snacks, and others even opened restaurants. The camp slowly became an actual community with a local economy. The ones who owned these businesses didn't want to leave, and it became apparently clear because they kept delaying their interview appointments to leave for the United States. Other refugees started mingling with the Filipino locals, and some even intermarried with them. The vendors at the Philippine markets did not treat the refugees any differently than the people living there. They were always joking around with Mr. Lee and his friends, even inviting them for drinking sessions at their shops. Mr. Lee always loved the fact that Filipino shop-owners offered them free beer so they could continue the party, or when some restaurant owners would pay for their meals after a good conversation. Talking and drinking with the locals was how Mr. Lee drastically improved his English.

The people from the PRPC would give the refugees ingredients for food every day which they had to cook for themselves. In Mr. Lee's building, there was a kerosene stove, but with all the other families living with them, one wasn't enough. Mr. Lee noticed one day a pair of young refugees huddled around a boiling pot of water. They weren't using the stove; they were using a nearby electric outlet. There was a wire plugged into the outlet, with the other end exposing its smaller wires was wrapped around a metal spoon. The electricity coming from the outlet flowed through the wire heating the spoon which was pointed into the bowl, making the water boil. Mr. Lee, attempting to improve their invention, quickly revealed his naivety.

"I thought, maybe I could boil the water faster if I tied more spoons around the wire," he says.

So, he tried boiling water in the same manner. However, instead of having one spoon, he used five. He pointed the spoons into his water bowl, and then plugged the wire into the outlet. Then he heard a boom, and all the lights in the building turned off. As the residents of the building went downstairs to figure out what had caused the lights to go out, Mr. Lee hastily unplugged the wire, hid everything near a trash pile, and tried to hide his embarrassment as he waited outside with everyone for the maintenance crew.

Overall, the Philippines had been the happiness Mr. Lee was fighting so long for. It made all the hardship of leaving an uncertain but comfortable life in Phnom Penh worth the risk. It was a preview of what he could perhaps expect once he arrived in the United States. Mr. Lee said it best when trying to summarize his layover in paradise.

"I had many good times. I drank a lot of beer, and I went to the ocean."

Mr. Lee had never dressed this formally in his life. He had on a pair of khaki pants and a striped polo shirt. Guang insisted that all her kids look their best to signal a good first impression in their new home. Mr. Lee, regretting that he had bought a size too small in pants from Bataan, struggled to feel comfortable on the plane seat. Having to wear a seatbelt made things 10 times worse, no matter how much he loosened its grip on his waist. As soon as the flight attendants stopped checking on him, he immediately unbuttoned his pants and unfastened his seatbelt while wishing to be back on the beach, shirtless and in baggy shorts.

Claiming a seat by the window, Mr. Lee gazed out at the lush green background masked by the darkness of nighttime that was Guam. In just over 12 hours, Mr. Lee would be in sunny San Francisco, a new world across the Pacific. The plane was a Panam 747, and it held Cambodian, Vietnamese, and Laotian refugees, sprinkled along with a large number of

American tourists returning home from their vacations. Mr. Lee was anxious yet excited to start the final leg of his journey. The plane took off, and Mr. Lee closed his eyes and slowly drifted off to sleep. Not long afterwards however, Mr. Lee woke up to the sound of the pilot's voice over the intercom.

"This is your captain speaking. I apologize but the aircraft is experiencing some complications, and we must turn back and land."

Immediately there was nervous commotion among the passengers, especially from the refugees. How bad was this complication? Then Mr. Lee heard a Vietnamese woman panicking towards the back of the plane. The flight attendant was trying her best to reassure and calm her down, but her English echoed throughout the plane.

"I don't want to die! I want to see the U.S.A. first!"

Then Mr. Lee heard another passenger scream that there was a fire. The tension inside turned into a panic. Mr. Lee could barely process what was happening over all the talking, screaming, and crying. He turned to look at Guang and Seng who were seated in the two seats next to him. They both had calm demeanors, not adding to the panic. Despite her best efforts, Mr. Lee noticed that Guang still couldn't hold back tears.

Mr. Lee opened his window to see if he could pinpoint what the problem was. There was a bright orange glow toward the front of the plane, and all Mr. Lee could see was smoke billowing towards the back of the plane. The left wing had caught on fire.

"Passengers, please close your windows," the pilot on the intercom said. Mr. Lee followed the lead of his mother and older brother and stayed calm. Out of everything they had been through, this was just one more hurdle on their journey to reach the United States. Mr. Lee closed his eyes again.

That night back in Guam, all passengers on the flight received compensation from the airline company. First, they were treated to a fancy restaurant, all expenses paid. Everyone could tell who the refugees were, not because of the color of their skin, but because of their reactions when served a large portion of steak. While the American tourists smiled and politely thanked the servers, the refugees were rowdy as they rejoiced; it was as if they had never seen a portion of meat that big in their lifetime. It may have been true for some of them. Naturally, they were met with stares by the U.S. tourists, but the refugees didn't care.

The airline said they would pay for a night in a 5-star hotel, and that the passengers would board a new plane for San Francisco the next morning. Mr. Lee had a balcony view over the pool from his room, and he observed the ambiance below, reminding him of the chill beach days in Bataan. There was romantic music playing, and a handful of U.S. tourists were lounging in chairs or at the bar drinking. There was one family with their kids swimming in the pool. Suddenly, Mr. Lee heard what sounded like a stampede of wild horses. What came after were maybe 30-40 refugees all screaming, celebrating, and jumping into the pool.

"I just sat on top of the balcony chuckling, watching these rowdy Asians make fools of themselves. It was madness!" Mr. Lee and I burst with laughter, almost spitting out peanuts. "I don't blame their behavior though, I understand it very well," he says.

The next morning Mr. Lee flew to San Francisco, thankfully with no complications, and as much as he enjoyed his short time in Guam, he was ready to see the United States.

It was November 1981 when the plane touched down at the San Francisco International Airport. Mr. Lee, Guang, Seng, Bieng, and Guah would eventually reunite with Chang and Teng at Uncle Qiang's restaurant in Arkansas. Dak would arrive five years later with Heng. After the plane landed, the refugees were directed to a platform and picked up by a bus. The San Francisco night sky was bright with lights, and as the bus kept driving towards the city, all Mr. Lee could process was the fact that he made it. Meanwhile, in the distance where the bus would eventually pass through, welcoming him to his new home, were the shining lit-up arches of the Golden Gate Bridge. He thanked the evil for letting him live. He thanked the evil for a second chance at life.

EPILOGUE

WE'LL COOK FOR YOU
LIKE A FAMILY

MR. LEE'S FACE is illuminated by the light of his screen; otherwise the background in his bedroom is dark. He smiles throughout the Skype call, happy to see me as we haven't spoken in months. We give each other updates on our lives. Just a week prior, I passed my Capstone course for the Schedler Honors College after successfully defending *Thank the Evil* in a 20-minute presentation. I wish that I spoke in front of a live audience, and not in my bedroom on Zoom, wearing shorts and flip-flops below my suit-and-tie, but 2020 has definitely redefined what is considered normal. Meanwhile, after doing business for 17-and-a-half years, Mr. Lee sold Oriental Kitchen to another Conway restaurant owner.

"How are you enjoying retirement?" I ask.

"I'm just taking some time off and spending some time with the younger one and Amanda since I've been working so much... I don't want to call myself completely retired. I have some friends in the restaurant business who are calling for me to come visit and maybe help out." Mr. Lee continues. "My foot wasn't feeling well. I hurt my ankle pretty bad, man. I think Amanda told you."

"I've been in bed for three weeks before I could start walking around again." Mr. Lee chuckles. "I have no idea how I hurt it. I think I twisted it in when I was in the Navy, and then after that the pain comes back every few years. Maybe I wasn't careful or something and twisted it again. The doctor took an x-ray and said everything looked fine. All he did was give me a shot. The pain is manageable now as long as I don't do any prolonged standing or heavy lifting."

Despite the foot pains and the impact of COVID-19 on small businesses throughout the country, Mr. Lee had already considered moving on from the restaurant business while I was interviewing him in 2019. I assumed Mr. Lee was forced to sell because of the pandemic, but apparently Oriental Kitchen didn't struggle. Business was booming.

At first Oriental Kitchen had to adjust. The first two weeks of stay-at-home orders were the hardest. The out-of-state supplier started to delay deliveries, and food costs increased.

Since many larger dine-in restaurants had to close down, it became impractical to send multiple trips of 18-wheelers to deliver a quarter of the supplies. The restaurant also installed plexi glass on the open rectangular frame to protect Mrs. Lee. They bought PPEs like masks, gloves, and face-shields. At the same time, customers and regulars kept coming in, increasing sales 15-20%. My mind wanders back to the initial quarantine when Amanda sent me Snapchats of all the order tickets they had to fill. Mr. Lee says there were nights where he arrived home past midnight. Despite record-breaking success in sales, the inconsistencies of the supplier compounded with the increased workload became an unbearable hassle, so the Lees closed Oriental Kitchen from June to August. Once they reopened, the restaurant stayed busy, Mr. Lee's foot began to hurt, and the owner of Conway's China Town approached him as a buyer. Mr. Lee finally found an owner with restaurant experience to carry on Oriental Kitchen's legacy, and now he suddenly has plenty of time on his hands.

"Most of the time I just stay and relax in bed. I still don't want to put too much pressure on my foot. I like to watch these YouTube videos sometimes about people travelling, eating street food and walking around. It's cool because I can explore all that world stuff from home."

"Sometimes Amanda drives me around just so I'm not always in the house, and if my foot is feeling fine I walk on the trail. Not much going on… just trying to avoid contact with a lot of people as you know, to stay safe and healthy."

Next I ask Mr. Lee to reflect on his time at Oriental Kitchen and how he managed to build a large customer base.

"I never paid a penny for advertising. Could you believe that?"

No, I couldn't.

Mr. Lee described the first month of business as incredibly slow. However, as time passed, business steadily grew until Oriental Kitchen received a consistent flow of hungry customers. Although the new owner wanted to put up a sign advertising the restaurant, Mr. Lee explained to him that if he continued operating the restaurant well, there wouldn't be a need for advertising. All of the regulars were from inside town, and social media makes spreading the word that much easier. It's also free.

"What made Oriental Kitchen stand out over other Asian restaurants in the city?" I asked.

Mr. Lee referred to his restaurant's slogan: We'll Cook For You Like Family. "Besides my family, that's where I spent my time, at Oriental Kitchen. I mean… I never treated Oriental Kitchen as a place just to make food and sell it to customers.

I treated it like I'm going there to cook food for the people I loved the most. Every day that I went there, I just did my best."

"I give all the credit to my customers. I hardly saw them since I was at the back, but I could feel their presence… and it put pressure on me to perform and provide the best possible meal, so that when they brought it home to their families, they wouldn't say that it sucks."

"I learned the tricks of cooking Chinese food from my partner when I worked at Fu Lin [another local restaurant]. Then I created my own recipes. My philosophy was to make sure the food was always fresh and that my kitchen was always clean. I spent hours after closing to clean. The Health Department inspector even came one time and told me she couldn't find anything wrong."

Mr. Lee taught me that nothing in life came easy. After surviving a genocide, one would think the human struggle would end. However, Mr. Lee and his wife continued to fight and work long hours in the grueling food service industry. In my eyes, learning how to climb palm trees and make *athuy* in order to survive a genocide should have been Mr. Lee's greatest achievement, but to him, it is the small Chinese-takeout restaurant connected to a gas-station that he has built and maintained for 17-and-a-half years.

As the whole world continues to grapple with the COVID-19 pandemic, your words and your story became more prevalent to me personally. To be content with what you have. To be generous to those who are struggling. To thank the evil that I am still alive despite living through tough times. Mr. Dereck Lee, thank you for allowing me to write your story. Truly, it was an honor and a pleasure.

PHOTOS

Family Photo 1967

As pictured left to right: Bieng, Chang, Gia, Guang,
Guah, Dak, Mr. Lee, Seng, Teng, Heng

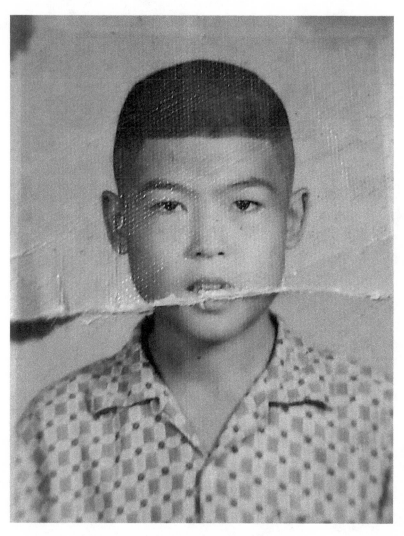

A young Mr. Lee in 1967.

Philippines

Philippines

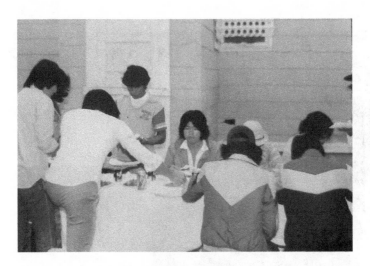

Texas Job Corps 1982

Florida U.S. Navy 1987

Featured on the Log Cabin Democrat (1997)

BIBLIOGRAPHY

Burgos, Sigfrido, and Sophal Ear. "China's Strategic Interests in Cambodia: Influence and Resources." *Asian Survey* 50, no. 3 (2010): 615–39.https://doi.org/10.1525/as.2010.50.3.615.

Calkins, Laura M. "Vietnamese Troops Withdraw from Cambodia." In *Salem Press Encyclopedia*. Salem Press, 2019.

Drivas, Peter G. "The Cambodian Incursion Revisited." *International Social Science Review* 86, no. 3/4 (June 2011): 134–59.

Duffy, Terence. "Toward a Culture of Human Rights in Cambodia." *Human Rights Quarterly* 16, no. 1 (1994): 82–104. https://doi.org/10.2307/762412.

Dunst, Charles. "U.S. Returns Ex-Refugees To Cambodia, Which Resists: [Foreign Desk]." New York Times, Late Edition (East Coast); New York, N.Y. December 13, 2018, sec. A.

Hays, Jeffrey. "CHINESE IN SOUTHEAST ASIA | Facts and Details." Accessed October 29, 2019. http://factsanddetails.com/asian/cat66/sub418/item2729.html#chapter-1.

Him, Chanrithy. *Growing Up under the Khmer Rouge: When Broken Glass Floats*. New York W.W. Norton & Company Inc, 2000.

Joint Committee on Southeast Asia. *Revolution and Its Aftermath in Kampuchea: Eight Essays*. Yale University Southeast Asia Studies, 1983.

Kiernan, Ben. *The Pol Pot Regime*. Yale University, 1996.

Marshall, Grant N, Terry L Schell, Marc N Elliott, S Megan Berthold, and Chi-Ah Chun."Mental Health of Cambodian Refugees 2 Decades after Resettlement in the United States." *JAMA* 294, no. 5 (August 3, 2005): 571–79.

Moise, Edwin E. "THE ROAD TO FREEDOM: A History of the Ho Chi Minh Trail." *Pacific Affairs* 79, no. 3 (Fall 2006): 558–59.

Normand, Roger. "The Teachings of Chairman Pot." *Nation* 251, no. 6 (August 27, 1990): 198.

O'lemmon, Matthew. "Buddhist Identity and the 1973 Cambodian Buddhist Holy War." *Asian Anthropology (1683478X)* 10 (August 2011): 121–38. https://doi.org/10.1080/1683478X.2011.10552607.

Owen, Taylor. "Bombs Over Cambodia." *The Walrus*, October 2006. Accessed October 1, 2019. https://thewalrus.ca/2006-10-history/.

Peang-Meth, Abdulgaffar. "A Study of the Khmer People's National Liberation Front and the Coalition Government of Democratic Kampuchea." *Contemporary Southeast Asia* 12, no. 3 (1990): 172-185. http://www.jstor.org/stable/42707623.

Ponchaud, Francois. *Cambodia: Year Zero*. New York, Holt, Rinehart and Winston, 1978.

Pran, Dith., Kiernan, Ben., and DePaul, Kim. *Memoirs by Survivors: Children of Cambodia's Killing Fields*. Chiang Mai, Thailand: Silkworm, 1997.

Schabas, William. Review of *Review of Genocide in Cambodia, Documents from the Trial of Pol Pot and Ieng Sary*, by Howard J. De Nike, John Quigley, and Kenneth J. Robinson. *Human Rights Quarterly* 23, no. 2 (2001): 470–77.

Schanberg, Sydney. *Beyond the Killing Fields*. Dulles, Virginia, Potomac Books Inc, 2010.

Shawcross, William. *Sideshow: Kissinger, Nixon and the Destruction of Cambodia*. New York: Simon & Schuster Inc, 1979.

Summers, Laura. "The Cambodian Civil War." *Current History, Inc* 63, (1972).

Tyner, James., & Cromley, Gordon. "Camps, cooperatives and the psychotopologies of Democratic Kampuchea." *Area* 50 (2018), 542-548. https://doi.org/10.1111/area.12423

Tyner, James A., and Stian Rice. "To Live and Let Die: Food, Famine, and Administrative Violence in Democratic Kampuchea, 1975–1979." *Political Geography*, SI: Violence and Space, 52 (May 1, 2016): 47–56. https://doi. org/10.1016/j.polgeo.2015.11.004.

Tyner, James. *From Rice Fields To Killing Fields: Nature, Life, and Labor under the Khmer Rouge.* Syracuse, New York: Syracuse University Press, 2017.

Vickery, Michael. *Cambodia: 1975-1982.* Boston, MA, South End Press, 1984.

Vries, Myra., and Weerdesteijn, Maartje. "The Life Course of Pol Pot: How his Early Life Influenced the Crimes He Committed." *Amsterdam Law Forum* 10, no. 2 (2018).

Wegner, Daniel M. "Try Not Think of a White Bear." *Psychology Today; New York*, June 1989.

Wright, George. "Cannibalism, Khmer Rouge and Horrors of War." The Cambodia Daily, April 25, 2015. https://english. cambodiadaily.com/news/cannibalism-khmer-rouge -and-horrors-of-war-82653/.

ABOUT THE AUTHOR

KENNY DURAN IS a Filipino-American immigrant who has resided in Little Rock, Arkansas for the majority of his life. His love of travelling and trying new cuisines stems from occasional family trips back to the Philippines. He spends his free time reading, over-analyzing TV shows, and spending time with the people he cares about the most. As an undergraduate at the University of Central Arkansas, he has earned a B.S. of Health Sciences while also graduating from the Schedler Honors College. Currently, he aspires to earn his Doctorate of Physical Therapy.

ACKNOWLEDGEMENTS

WRITING AND PUBLISHING *Thank the Evil* has proven to be a daunting, but ultimately rewarding process. First I would like to thank Dr. Jennifer Case for being my guide and mentor during the entirety of this book. As a novice writer, I felt at ease as she walked me through the process of writing creative nonfiction, critiqued my drafts, and informed me of my publishing options. I would also like to thank Pulaski Academy's Social Sciences Department Chair Mr. Bill Topich for fact-checking the manuscript and allowing me to borrow several books from his collection of Cambodian Genocide sources. Next I want to thank Caitlyn Phan for designing a stellar book cover and my dear friend Louisa Utley for being a meticulous copy editor. Lastly, I would like to thank the Lee family for being gracious hosts at Oriental Kitchen and to Mr. Lee who made this project possible. *Thank the Evil* serves as a memento to the triumph and relationships I have experienced throughout this journey.

CPSIA information can be obtained
at www.ICGtesting.com
Printed in the USA
BVHW081659220221
600776BV00007B/309

9 781736 334805